Under the Wings
of the Crow

Under the Wings of the Crow

A Legacy of Poems
New and Selected

Fran Claggett-Holland

Three Ravens

Everything in the world exists within the tip of a brush.
Lu Chi (261–303)

three ravens live
in the strokes
of the artist's brush

dreams live
in the shadowed wings
of three ravens

Ravens cast no
shadow
in the dark of the moon

moonlit ravens
give way to
pale shades of dawn

RiskPress

Published by RiskPress
100 Wildhorse
Santa Fe, NM 87506
(with the generous cooperation of fmsbw Press, San Francisco, California)

Published in the United States of America
Copyright © Fran Claggett-Holland, 2022

ISBN: 978-0-9848403-8-0

Front cover painting: "Heroic Crow"
Pat Cheal ©2021
oil on panel, 18" x 24"
www.pattheartist.com

Back cover painting: "Raven's Dream"
Eric G. Thompson ©2021
egg tempura, 24" x 19"

Book design:
Charlie Pendergast and Kevin Connor

Proceeds from all sales of this book will be given to
Sebastopol Center for the Arts
www.sebarts.org

Dedicated, as always, to
Madge Holland
September 11, 1927 - October 6, 2014
who accompanied me all this way and
who still inspires me to keep climbing.

memory begins in loss
with age we learn to live there
where we are young
where we will live
forever

"As if it had all the time in the world," the poet wrote of the ladybug climbing the screen. And I felt myself climbing from one small metal square to the next, upward, always upward, but pausing now and then to rest. That's how we lived our lives, isn't it, as if we had all the time in the world.

Today I sat on the floor by the tansu and opened the bottom drawer. envelopes filled with photographs, letters, cards. but mostly photos, ancient ones of your four grandparents (four! all living when we were all grown up.) I had had none since I was thirteen, but here, at thirty, you had four. So we smiled and said, you will live forever. I took your long life as my own, and knew that we were destined to grow old together. And we continued to climb up the screen door.

The screen has grown rusty. but the ladybug doesn't mind. She just keeps moving up, one step at a time. Oh we talked about growing old, but always together, always side-by-side on our screen door. Death was so far away, like the top of the door. We couldn't even see where we were going. We couldn't see the top.

Pictures spill out, pictures of you before I knew you. How could that be? Hadn't I always known you, known we would be sitting here together some day in the future, looking at the photographs of our life. But now I sit here surrounded by photos—pictures of us in Turkey, Egypt, China, Cambodia, Thailand. Hawaii, of course. One of the two of us heaving that great log into the bell, the deep ringing echoing through the trees forever. And envelope after envelope of our Afghan hounds, each one unlike any of the others, yet all our heartdogs, making way for the Salukis to come, and the irrepressible Whippet.

But I am sitting here for a purpose. I have paused in my upward journey. I am gathering photos that I will arrange into the pages that hold, between them, the words and pictures that belie that long ago belief... words that attest to our life, our life that continues, even after you have reached the top, going on ahead, but dropping back in a shadow image to accompany me the rest of the way.

Author's Preface

In every life there are details of memory that are left in shadow. These indistinct traces compel the writer in us, urge us forward completing images of place, person, event. They move us toward form, allowing silence to become a frame, for it is silence that gives shape to memory. The image, the line, the stanza, the word – all exist against a background of silence, creating dynamic tension between the writer and the reader. Filling this space is central to the act of both writing and reading. In this way, the reader becomes partner to the writer. Together we create the essential poem.

Introduction

Dear Reader,

Is it presumptuous for me to say "lucky you?" If you are reading this, you are holding Fran Claggett-Holland's book Under the Wings of the Crow, a collection of new and previously published poems forged from a sustained appreciation of all that illuminates the liminal spaces between mind and world. These poems crackle and shine. They are the artifacts of a life brilliantly lived.

In a passage of Rilke's Letters to a Young Poet, he advises, "As if no one had ever tried before, try to say what you see and feel and love and lose, …describe your sorrows and desires, the thoughts that pass through your mind and your belief in some kind of beauty—describe all these with heartfelt, silent, humble sincerity and, when you express yourself, use the things around you, the images from your dreams and the objects you remember." Fran Claggett-Holland's poems masterfully achieve all that Rilke has advised. Her poems embody what he wrote to his student, and like Rilke, Fran has taught and influenced countless numbers of young poets and some not so young.

In reading these poems you will find a multi-dimensional voice and a tangible presence of self. Being with Fran is like being with a Zen master, where there is always a transmission, be it about poetry or having a profound talent for living within the rich slipperiness of human nature.

I am blessed to know this remarkable woman and call her my dear friend. Well, I must say it again as you enter this book, "lucky you." Lucky me.

With love,

Les Bernstein

Foreword by Freeman Ng

Fran was the teacher who got me started writing poetry in high school. Her first book of poetry, Black Birds and Other Birds, was (along with a slim Selected Poems of T.S. Eliot) the first book of poetry I owned. Her poems in that book were (along with Eliot's Wasteland) the first poems I read, over and over, not for school but for my own pleasure. They have a seminal place in the development of my poetic imagination.

So I was thrilled to learn that Fran was coming out with this book of both new and selected old poems. Though I have all her other books and have read all her published – and many unpublished – poems, being asked to write this foreword led me to start looking at them not as individual books or poems that I loved, but collectively, as a single body of work.

Or at least trying to do so.

In the end, there was too great a breadth of theme and technique and subject matter (and perhaps too small a span of time or distance) for me to take it all in at once. So instead, I'm going to introduce you to this book by showing you three brief glimpses of the many Frans I was able to identify as I swept my gaze over the montage of her poetry.

Fran the mythmaker

In "Evolution of the Sun-Temple", a building and landscaping project conceived by Fran's life-partner Madge for their then Berkeley home is visited by a neighbor, a Nobel physicist and "aging giant of a mind," who proclaims it a Sun Temple. And this is in fact an aspect of Fran's genius: to discern, in the randomness of everyday life ("the blue Chinese prayer rug, / the hanging basket from Mexico, / the stained-glass window…the moss-green fence") the patterns of timeless myths and archetypes. Her poems frequently invoke figures from a wide assortment of mythologies that show her love of, and familiarity with, the heights and depths to which the human mind repeatedly returns in its attempts to understand itself. But she doesn't stop there.

The erudite neighbor "stump[s] off, satisfied," but the poet isn't quite. It's not that she rejects his muttered conclusion – the poem reports Madge responding, "That, too" in acceptance – but Fran goes on to make a myth or build an archetype of her own. The "circle of stone and cement" becomes The Circle, and is completed in lines that elevate it to a place beyond the accidental occurrences of the world.

...you finished the inner circle, emptying the
burlap bags of stones we had gathered from the beach
one by one, washed up by the tides for just this place
all these years later.

The loon from "Heron And Loon" (actually a heron, yes: "that, too")
occupies such a place in my mind. It's a figure as powerful as any Apollo
or Janus or Fool. And the Aunt in "Birth Memories" has an even greater
significance to me because that's the myth that Fran and I have adopted
with respect to each other: she my spiritual mother and I her son.

And it goes on and on:

> *The actual, scientific, Darwinian wolf in "Wolf Speaks in Myth",*
> *distinct from the storied Wolf of existing mythologies, rising to its own unique*
> *mythological niche entirely through its narration of that very eventuality.*

> *Two sheep in a photo, nudged toward the mythological by the subtly*
> *formalistic construction of "the power of the lifted hoof" in "What Is It about*
> *these mountain sheep?"*

> *The three "dawn redwoods" in "A Sense of Permanence" that are as*
> *totemic in their presence as any local god or spirit.*

Fran is much traveled in the "realms of gold." She often brings back
treasures from those lands as gifts for us readers. But sometimes, for a
special treat, she forges her own.

Fran the philosopher of the mind

It takes the sun —
> *rising*
> > > *or falling —*
> *to turn the white gull black.*
We must go colorblind
> *to see*
> > *the shape a wing makes.*

This ending of the titular poem from Black Birds and Other Birds is only
the beginning a long investigation by Fran in many of her poems into the
nature of perception and creativity, particularly by poets and

artists (which is to say: essentially by all humans). In an earlier draft of this foreword, I wrote that "we might some day be able to construct an ars poetica from fragments of her existing poems alone," but in this final draft, I've decided to just do it:

to walk
shifting sands
to probe
for tracings known only
by what
it touches defined
by what lies
beyond it takes
a careful eye

there is
a darkness
at the edge earth
silence space
for silence moving out
of silence sight
beyond the dark

there must
be a way and then
the very land oasis
of stones reshaping
everything familiar shadow
of a poem branch
of tomorrow
drops
into the room

Fran the human

Finally, I come to an aspect of Fran's poetry that surprised me as I reread the poems in this book. This might sound strange to you, and I would agree. Fran's heart – her warmth, her empathy, her love – is probably the first thing most people notice about her and her poetry. Yet, I had to be reminded of it.

I suspect it's because I think of her primarily as teacher and mother.

Now, though, after rereading the many poems in which she celebrates her relationships with others, consoles them over their losses, suffers loss herself, speaks directly with her dead, I'm most happy to consider her my friend.

> As I said, these are just three views of Fran. There are many others: Fran the sage, Fran the oracle, Fran the naturalist. Fran the teacher, the imagist, the chronicler of moments – just for a start. More natures than any god and more faces than any hero. You can begin meeting them – or reminding yourself of their uncontainable multiplicity – by turning the page.

Contents

Under Raven Wing
Book I

Three Braided Poems by Les and Fran
Braided poems are poems written by two people,
in this case by Les Bernstein and Fran Claggett-Holland

Black Birds and Other Birds
Book II

Crow Crossings
Book III

The Consciousness of Stone
Book IV

Under Raven Wing
Book I

In Times Like These

In Times like These,
It is Necessary to Talk about Trees.
Adrienne Rich

I
In Times Like These

Listen.
        You are overwhelmed.
        You are unprepared.
        You are terrified.
        But open the window.
        Listen to the voices outside.
        They have gathered there.
        Your mothers your daughters
        Your nieces. Your sons.
        Yes, your sons and most
        clear most articulate
        most anguished---
        your sisters.
Put out your hand,
Let yourself be led
Away from the window
        toward the door.

Listen, outside
        you will hear the trees
        you will hear the wind in the aspen
        you will notice the silver undersides
            of the poplar leaves.
Listen to the sounds of these trees.
Listen to Daphne tell of what she learned
        as a laurel tree.

II
Daphne speaks

I once lived among the waters —
the rivers, the springs
a tidepool at the bottom of a waterfall.
My father Peneus, the river god
protected me from lustful Apollo

1

now my leaves bend to the wind
and I listen to the aspen, the poplar
these trees too have known
the waters of life

in this time of
cosmic upheaval
remember when you
were born of water and
ran with the naiads
along rivers and oceans

when you emerged
from mother earth you
like me were overwhelmed
terrified unprepared
for life without the
cool waters.

Life as a tree
gives stability and
communion
between earth and sky
My leaves change
and fall as I navigate
my world

listen
In these times
imagine possibility
walk the sands that surround you
notice the small

the sea anemone
affixed to rock in its watery home
see how it spreads its tendrils
of pale lapis and deep magenta
shades between those of the artist's palette

step into the tidepool
reclaim the waters of your birth

look to the frog
 how it moves
    the gathering in
        the leap
            the landing—
limbs folded
            silent as stone

This Consciousness that is Aware

I

hearing his voice
again and again
as I heard it the first time
long before I knew him
long before I had any idea of the meaning

of the words   his high frenetic voice
stunned me with knowledge
so dark and deep and vast
I fell into the power and beauty
of primordial myth

I do not analyze the fabric of those
stirrings, hearing the unending rapture
of language, of poetry, of myth
encompassing everything I knew
and everything I did not yet know

always I am permitted to return
to his meadow and know it for the first time
know again the poem that became the falconress
conveying the ecstasy
of ultimate pain

waking now to the end of my beginning
I measure out my days
grounded in rhythm and rhyme
grounded in deep structure--
in this consciousness of form

II

with earth as his easel what fibers
make up his cavern-splitting brush
what plants secrete ink for the greens
oranges reds and browns
that cover his crumbling palette

what of the sky, day or night
constellations or stars, moon or sun
not to be diminished by these

rumbling monoliths of steel energy
in the hand of this earth-wielding artist

what draws us to this art
that cannot be hung on gallery walls
familiar art encompassing space
designed for the intimate views
of Vermeers and Leonardos

we could understand Christo
who added fabric to the natural world,
who covered expectations with a white surprise
and we drove at dusk to see the
moon rising over every fluttering hill to the sea

but this—the moving of mountains
creating craters to emulate canyons
this re-forming of our world
is re-shaping everything familiar
the very land under our feet

III

when is my body
going to admit
it cannot rise and shine
with the sun hidden
in a wrap of heavy cloud
and every step tentative
on this wet sheen of cement

when am I going to believe
in the continuity of all
we used to know without
thought or anxiety
about sending our children
off to school for lessons
in what to do when

when
when
when is this land
this earth, this
earth-shattering
unstable

atmosphere
we are living in
going to listen
to the poets
the artists
going to
settle
into
form

A Branch of Tomorrow

memory begins in loss
with age we learn to live there
where we are young
where tomorrow will live
forever

this is what I wanted for the last poem
the poet writes
as a branch of tomorrow
from the redwood tree
drops
into the room

We see this green branch
fall gently across the grain
the wood not long ago
part of another tree, the table
top sanded and polished
sides with jagged memory

but the green branch of tomorrow
almost in our hands
changes everything
The poet says,
We are close
enough to childhood,
so easily purged
of whatever we thought we were to be

we thought
we knew where we stood

gathered there
in the room
around this table where
our stories have been
twice told

we see the dream of our childhood
filled with remembrances of earlier lives
forgotten as we grew but now
remembering
the sun-god's white-domed temple
the endless sands
of the Bedouin desert
and we feel the pull of Demeter
who shadowed us
through these many lives

the edge of our belief is just beyond
this life we are living with dreaming eyes
we gather up our stories
rich with sighthounds and white ravens
knowing
the branch of tomorrow
is built on today
lying ready
the poet says
to bud forth

When Our Greatest Fears of Yesterday Become Transmogrified

I
The First Fires

In the middle of yet another winter storm:
the fence is tight and holding. If it buckles,
falls, my sighthounds would follow their bent
and streak out into danger. The fence
is my greatest fear during these winter storms.
I look out the far window to check on the trees,
three gigantic redwoods, standing firm
with intent on remaining upright, so close
to this house they protect, even in
this relentless onslaught of water. Their roots,
I understand, are shallow.

Just yesterday, it seems, we were in the
reverse, a drought, forbidding any unjustifiable
use of water. "Use grey water to keep the plants
alive. Take short showers. Go out to eat
but do not request the obligatory glass of water. "

Now all is changed. A flood warning invades
my smart phone. Piercing its way into my brain,
the alarm takes me to the windows once again.
Check fence, trees.

Checking, checking, checking.

II
Three Years Later

The side fence has rotted out and is being
replaced. Board by board, it takes shape,
elegant redwood straight and tall,
but there is no fear now of winter storms.
No fear of drought ahead although we have
had scant rain and summer is upon us.
The fear of fire lurks with memories of
last year's evacuation, but even those have
faded and become almost unrecognizable.
The dogs rarely leave the comfort of their
beds, but clearly miss their daily walks.

Today we know there is no fence against
the threat that keeps us isolated,
each alone in our sequestered state,
and when we must leave our sheltered
space, we become the aliens we used to fear,
the spiked corona so beautiful in the abstract,
so deadly in the body.

We do not check the trees, we trust the new fence.
We take our temperature, wash our hands,
don the masks that muffle our speech,
measure the distance between us.

Checking, checking, checking.

Tabula Rasa

Children are no longer taught
to write cursive. That beautiful hand of my father's,
no less impressive when he signed a check
as when he signed his letters and reports.
And my mother's hand, learned the Palmer way,
"move your hand from the elbow," she told me,
demonstrating on the kitchen table.
I could never even approximate her beautiful script
now preserved, along with my father's love letters
in the trunk in my garage.

Letter after letter, back and forth,
they wrote, passionate and private, never imagining
their children would one day sit and read them aloud,
marveling at their youth, their ardor, their
carefully drawn words, their own calligraphy.

A hundred years later, my brother and I,
sitting at the old round oak table,
read in tandem, words of passion, of love,
of forever, written by these two strangers,
our parents.

adagio cantabile

sometimes memory isn't really memory at all
it starts off that way, but underneath it is
the what-if of your life

you write about the way you played
Beethoven when you were fifteen
but really you

are writing about what if you were still
playing Beethoven, the Pathetique
the second movement

which cast such a spell over everyone
they closed their eyes and came
close to floating

leaving the old upright there
where it stood in the dining room
with you dazed and floating too

and everyone humming the familiar
melody of your childhood
translated into the

reality of your fifteen-year-old self
alone on the stage of every
recital you were ever in

and your mother and father
and brothers and aunts and even
Beethoven himself

smiling as you whisper
is this the way you hear it
now that you are deaf

and he nods and the tears
come and he sits down beside me
and puts his hands over mine

Surrounded by Beauty

I never thought about growing up
beautiful or not; It didn't enter
into my consciousness.

being or not being beautiful
was not a thought I remember
ever having. I was never compared

by my mother to other children
I always had beautiful clothes
They just were. My mother made them

As I grew up, I did recognize
that I had a big nose. One day
I said in a friend's house

When I grow up, I might have my
nose fixed. The younger sister of my
friend looked at me and cried

Oh no, then you wouldn't be you!
I was shaken by her insistence
and never gave the idea further thought.

A Sense of Permanence

the first house
three dawn redwoods
a bulwark
in front of the house
a magical protection

they stood as redwoods do
straight and tall
drawn to a silent drumming
we looked closely
found acorns secreted

woodpeckers
burrowing their future
where it lies
untouched by wind
rain or season

now this last house
three ancient redwoods
reenact their
heritage of long ago
bear witness

to the lives that have come
and the lives
that will go
untouched by moon
or season

Wallace Stevens Speaks of Degrees of Reality

and are there, then,
degrees of reality

what is real after all
is it what I
see

       (the first green on the hill
           we see from the deck)
taste

       (the lemon from our own tree
           the hint of cardamom)
hear

       (the morning call of the raucous raven
           at the top of our persimmon tree)
feel

       (the touch of your hand
           first thing in the morning)

but what about
all that I know
and can no longer perceive
through eye, ear, hand
       (the perpetual sound
           of the ocean by the shed
           we built on the cliff)

and what did Heisenberg say
that the observation itself
       altered what we looked at
       changed it
so what I see as
Mediterranean blue
       (oh definitely blue)
is a wine-dark sea
       to Homer

what is truth then
what beauty
are they both
       degrees of reality

Evolution of the Sun-Temple

It began in the mind, the circle
that would both enclose and project the eye.
Reality, weeds. Knee high,
stickery weeds. In the mind
a smooth circle.

Even the approach is different.
The first glimpse, dropping
down the steep place in the road, shows
the moss-green irregular circle
enclosing space, bringing it into the house,
extending it beyond.

Reality, a water-tank across the road.
In the mind, a fence, just high enough
to obscure the tank, preserve the bank
of eucalyptus trees.

Reality, joggers and drivers, peering
in through glass walls, strangers' eyes
lighting on the blue Chinese prayer rug,
the hanging basket from Mexico,
the stained-glass window
catching and changing the sun.
In the mind, the moss-green fence,
joggers and cars reduced to eyeless sound.

The base, a circle of stone and cement
radiating out in arcs. Round piling posts,
washed green, sunk into earth. Then the
rough lumber sawed, curved, each board
cut to fit in one place only. Panels rising,
grooved, stained.

The Circle, you called it
until the neighbor, a Nobel physicist,
walked his dog into the half-finished space.
Sun-temple, he muttered, aging giant of a mind,
poking around, examining, eye to microscope,
stumping off, satisfied.

That, too, you said,
as you finished the inner circle, emptying the

burlap bags of stones we had gathered from the beach
one by one, washed up by the tides for just this place
all these years later.

The Predicament of Being Human

Fear and worry born of love
leave us easily distracted
by the overlay of memory —
the thin palimpsest
that almost reveals the painting
we live with day after day

it is raining lightly as we follow
the artist's stream between
 grey cliffs and ragged fence
brush moving toward the pale
orange sunclouds just past
the final stand of trees

there miraculously the world bursts open
we trade the axis of rain and cold
for sun-heavy warmth that
never quite reaches the stone
pushing against the ribs —
the still beating heart

Ekphrastic Poem for a Warren Bellows painting

just human after all

It was no surprise
to see the monster there
made human by your art
the cyclops I had always thought
to be strange and fearful
fair game for Odysseus's clever
ploy was suddenly pathetic with
his one misplaced eye
which in another culture gave him
special visionary talent
or later finding Lady Macbeth
lamenting that she would carry
Duncan's blood on her hands forever
and Medea casting her spell
on the amoral Jason with his
golden fleece and making sure
their innocent children never
lived to know the wickedness
of their fabled father
oh, the monsters are ever with us
beside us inside us reminding us
that to be human requires more
than history more than myths more
than the gods would have us know.

punctuation dies on the page

vowels in retreat
consonants
do the work

tadpoles disappear
space
grows on the blank page

questions are redundant
what is beauty
what truth

periods
blacken the rice paper
bamboo leaf leans

a hundred leaves
the frog leaps
death —a flourish

To the poet who asked for help in revising

Whose poem is this, she asks,
looking at my words stretched and
separated and scratched out while
other words foreign to me were inserted
and lines moved around up and down
always with a maybe or a question mark
as if there were no intention for them not
to replace or recast or reshape the words
in my original.

My tanka master speaks in my ear:
if only one word of the original remains,
the poem is yours. But remember
if the poem is yours, you are responsible
for its final form. Feel free to disregard the
insertions, the changes, but above all,
give each possibility your full consideration.
Accept changes with grace if they improve
the original. Stand firm in your knowledge.

It is, after all, your poem.

At the Asilomar Conference: Tarot after Dinner

I held my breath, stopped shuffling the cards,
knew what I was waiting for: the call.
Voices that had been expectant suddenly
silenced as the grey-eyed nun stood,
stiff and unyielding by my side.

Knowing I had no choice, I turned
the first card. Significator.
She took my eye. She was the card.
The High Priestess. Of course. No other
would dare manifest in this cell.

And then I ran, leaving the sanctuary,
the haven of my heaven on earth,
hearing the splintering of the doors, the
crackling of the windows the stained
glass portraying salvation; I ran

tearing myself from the god who had
promised safety knowing there was
no refuge from the fire and the soldiers
pummeling this wooden structure
deep in the wooded forest

breathing the heat of the fire
that replaced the cold of the stones
running from centuries of dread
from the spectre of paramount
authority, still she stood

guarding the door, the white-robed
mother superior unblemished
as her habit, standing,
compelling me to read the cards
that lay before me once again

 I felt the calm gaze
of Sister Katherine, who
without compassion but with full
knowledge of the outcome
said, unsmiling... "Read."

Terror in the dust

Terror in the dust
Terror staring back at you
There is the terror of not getting it right of
trying to make the words true of
listening to the truth of
the heart
the spirit
the body
the mind
of finding the truth that does not violate any of them
that does not violate the
spirit of the word
set down
revised
deleted
added back
transformed again and again while
the terror of the not-truth
still stares up at you saying
That is not what I meant at all. That is not it, at all.

A Light in the Dark

There is a darkness
at the edge of sight
the more you look
out of the corner of your eye
the more you fade away

When you fade away
others see you the way
you once were
at the edge of night
beyond the corner of their eye

There is a light beyond the dark
a light at the very edge
of sight a light straight on
when only you can see
around the corner of your life

What is it about these mountain sheep?

What is it about these
shaggy mountain sheep
that holds my heart
in abeyance

sheep I have never seen
but a photographer I know
a man whose vision
expands my own

he saw in these sheep
the power of the lifted hoof

how is it that he can give to me
the eye of knowledge
sacred to these sheep
who live their lives

poised on the edge
of awareness

After Reading Ocean Vuong

naked poems
nuked poems
naked as the night
that bore them screaming
from all the mothers from your own mother in the land of your birth
naked poems nuked
by soldiers that thrust their heritage on you
mirrored
in every lake you see

oh narcissus
are you not beautiful
with your bloodred arms
wrapped around every dying dolphin your father held
his own blood running free disappearing in the water
on its way to the
ocean
your name
and your
narrative

For Adrianne, whose book *Morgan* lies unread

It has been a day of waiting,
a day without spells,
a day of not knowing.

The light is yellowed with hope and fear,
not with sun, a fire burning
just beyond the hill we know is there,
there where she, Morgan Le Fay,
cast her spell on the book you wrote
never to be published, but living
in the ambiguity of
reality and ethereality.
Living in words written
but never read.
As if to read it would break
the bond you had, you
and Morgan,
beyond her childhood
with her brother Wart,
later Arthur,
beyond her teacher Merlin,
found again in the magic
we carried
on the small boat
to your grave,
the book still unread,
the watery beyond
filled with pages and pages
armloads of roses
from your garden
your final spell.

Canis Major III: In Transition

the wolfdog draws near
the fire our forebears
built at the edge
of the river
she is heavy with her burden

above, almost out of hearing
a high reedy droning
startles
she searches the sky

head back, the grey wolfdog
bays at the night—
at the unfamiliar
sound above, intruder
on a world newly
generating fire

intertwined with the smoke
the scent of wild boar
draws her closer
her pups will need
food

she skirts the flame
twigs crackling
to fire
to the delicate
foot-holding
shadow of her
and our future

for now—
a pregnant
silence

Wolf Speaks in Myth

Years ago I assumed a guise,
grandmother of that child.
Careless, to be so fooled.
Another time, I guarded a child.
Her parents, trusting.
Coming home, they saw the blood.
Shot an arrow into my heart.
Then, hearing a cry, the baby
safe in her crib.
They never saw the bear.

Those early humans
sat in a circle around the magic
of their new discovery.
Skirting the fire and the people,
I stood at the edge. They were hungry.
Above, my friend the raven circled,
taking me to a kill. Tentative,
I shared my dinner with the people.
The wise ones saw the connection:
raven, fire, wolf, food.

Today, I am hunted, feared,
by the new people.
My hunting ground is small.
The raven hunts
in ever-widening circles.
I look now to the people
who remember, who know
I am the one who became
their desert hounds, their
afghans, their salukis.
who, with the raven,
brought them food.
I wait for the time when
Raven and Woman and I
will be the genesis
of a new story.
A new myth.

On the Eve of Autumn

Emily described for us
a certain slant of light
those many moons ago.
Here, on the equinox of summer
we glimpse its shadow.

We may talk of returning to
whatever normal was,
as if perpetual summer were
attainable, even as we know
those heady moments are memory.

We have always known
the words, but not the melody
of the emerging dusk of life,
this singular beauty that marks
the eve of autumn.

Now we begin to savor
the lengthening infringement
of the hint of winter,
this shadowing under
a fragmentary sun.

Winter Solstice:
Persephone's Return

I stand at my kitchen window
in the silence of the still sleeping
house and watch the sun
scatter eucalyptus light into leaves,
peel red strips of sky from
smoothed trunks.
Naked in the morning.

Gathering up the shards of light,
I arrange them into day, work,
and they emerge
into sudden brilliance.
Jays flash blue glints.
The sun warms my back.

The winter garden grows green,
all leaves. A single turnip
purples the earth where I dig
into clumped earth, press clay,
mold the vessel that gathers the rain.
The birds drink from the earthen moon.

Evening, I hold the water-colored
sky bowl in my hands, descend
as daughter of the earth, and dream,
as the moon rises, tipping
the bowl, awakening to each return
of the day with crimson lips,
pomegranate seeds
still on my tongue.
When it grows light,
I will plant them.

Flickering Lights

I would write a poem for you
a poem without time or distance
a poem hidden in a potted orchid
above a yellow and lavender tablecloth
about to blossom

the rose clings to the petaled earth
dark chocolate supports
a flotilla of marshmallows
distortions of reality
animate moons

in this small yard
no walnut husks or persimmons
hang on black boughs
no trace of ice on this deck
to note the prints of afghan hounds
marking the day that snow
obscured November

I would write a poem for you
a poem without time or distance
but look
the lights you hung
on the fence
still flicker silently
until the sun turns them off

Aubade for the Quiet House

I awaken to a still-dark room
No sound to acknowledge a new day
No sense of the dream that woke me

The silent saluki across my feet
is, like me, not moving but awake
His eyes as always awaiting my move

Was it like this yesterday
and the day before
dreamless dark and silent

Will it be like this tomorrow
or will we be able to move freely
call out an aubade to the morning

Open to what once was as natural
as the sun falling across your face
as natural as another day of living

Until

Your story is not my story.
Your dog is not my dog.
You loved your dog
He was the best dog in your world.
I loved my dog.
He was the best dog in my world.

We grew old.
I had to keep living.
He wouldn't know what to do without me.
I had to keep living so he would keep living.
That's how it was.

Suddenly he grew old faster.
As did I.

One day he just laid down and died.
As did I.

My dog is not your dog.
Still, your story is not my story.

Until it is.

In and Out of Time

Rooted but not bound
floating in the subtle
wind of color
that portends
deafening maelstroms
where the bird
of myth and poetry
wings erasing the sun
flies beyond sound
above this momentary
island where we live
deep in blue feathery
fathoms

The Fool, Again

I have written my last poem about the Fool,
androgenous avatar of life
contemplating death
contemplating life after death.
That is my life now, Fool,
letting the Magician with all the
suits show their power—

the pentacle, feet planted
firmly in the teeming earth,
the sword of the mind showing
both sides of the insightful blade.
The rod shifty, but the cup
stabilizes the heart, keeps it pulsing
beyond earthly limits.

Oh, Magician, I have felt your absence,
waited for your all-knowing,
all-seeing gaze of absolution.
When my heart slows and stops
then I will know the merger
is complete.

At Death

I

an unbroken egg
the yolk suspended in its ocean

a white curtain fluttering
at the bedside of a child

the milk flowing out of
Vermeer's pitcher

the vermillion of the hummingbird
outside the diningroom window

her unlined face a perfect oval
against the enveloping fire opal tapestry

II

on writing the poem
that fell into my fingers

who is to say
this word or that

the word
always the word

the words fall
unpredictably

Vermeer
vermillion

who could know to write
them in conjunction

who could know
this was to be

a poem about death
a poem about her death

and about my grandmother's death
all those years ago

a death I never witnessed
but knew

as she never knew Vermeer
but knew the hummingbird

that laid her eggs
unbroken

in the tiny nest that appeared
on the same limb of the same tree

year after year
disappearing after the young

flew into the cerulean sky
as did she

THREE BRAIDED POEMS

Braided poems are poems written by two people,
In this case by Les Bernstein and Fran Claggett-Holland

A Journey Lighted by the Aurora Polaris

15 Chinese Elephants are on a long march north
and no one knows why

New York Times, June 2021

forget the fallen
embrace the risen
the unexpected vision
exposes the hidden

beyond village and farmland
fifteen great lumbering endlings
move in heavy unrelenting folds
through the wrinkled gray

a fallen industrial world tatters ties
an unwarranted lacuna
stalls the engine of the ordinary--
distance is now the imperative

singularity names them all
provides remembered diasporas
a heightened sense of new well being
a buffer of shared belonging

admit the hidden path to Polaris
guidance transmitted silently
by delicate vibrations whispered
into the elephant ear

Emily as High Priestess

an anarchy of experience
piles up in my brain
the high priestess of poetry
has no mercy

strobe after strobe dazzle
logic dazes into communion
my rewired mind
dashing everywhere

a scandal of artistic eruption
reveals Pompeii where
people frozen mid-gesture
resume normality

how is it that this priestess
lives in an arcane world
where that thing with feathers
is caught in the maw of inevitable

Measuring the Dark

when the heavens empty
and stars restless and roaming
ignite bright white light
with no reflection
shimmering the edges
abstractions fall
as geometries of
attention waver
between the mind
and the heart

rendered to a human scale
the perceived universe
like a quarter moon
insists on keeping
the mind's minimal light
awake
through the absence
of all it once knew

how do we measure
these too bright
too illuminated nights
in our overcrowded
fragile vessel
the dark engendered
hard longings of soul

within our smaller perimeter
the heart's valiant efforts
may fizzle and wilt
and yet
the pilot light
glows
warm and steady

Black Birds and Other Birds
Book II

Reverie

A lovely day is like a music box
wound up at break of dawn which never fades.
When homeward come the slowly driven flocks
of gentle sheep, the evening serenades
replace the lighter gayer melodies
of Re's domain; that brilliant charioteer
of sunny song gives way to rhapsodies
of Cynthia; to her is bent the ear
of each nocturnal creature. Calm, serene
contentment settles o'er the restful lands
in strains of mystic chords. With lowly mien
the humble creatures sleep to starry strands.
Thus Morpheus with his dulcimer holds sway
Until the morn doth bring another day.

Mary Frances Claggett, 1947
Senior in high school; obviously a Latin student

Black Birds and Other Birds

It is not enough to know
   the birds
         only at noon.

At noon you say
      see, it is a tern,
   I know it by its red beak,
           or
      look, the gull has
   grey wings,
         or still again,
      the blackbird has frightened
         the purple finch.

At noon, we know a thing
         by its color.
It takes the sun —
    rising
          or falling —
  to turn the white gull black.
We must go colorblind
   to see
      the shape a wing makes.

Janus Bird

Mythology does not tell me that the crow
      cawing in January winds
      heralds the two-faced god,

The crow breaks over the dunes
      scattering the shorebirds
      with a sudden cry
         then stands
   alone on the rain dark sand
      black-etched mirror of the lonely god
      destined always to be looking
         in the other direction.

As the Crow Flies

I.

Is it that the crow
        chooses always
    the bare
            bleached
    limb of the
            dead tree

Or is it that I
    cannot see him
            unless he is
                there?

II.

    When I saw the crow
I was sure that the other
    had been a raven.

III.

    from here to there
(on taking your measure
    from the flight
of a pelican)

    Some distances
cannot be measured
    as the crow flies.

Morning at Bodega Bay

What is surprising every time
What you never get used to
or prepared for   is the
    raven   flashing out from its
                    towering cliff depression
                    full across your face
    as you descend   in the morning
to the sea.
                                                35

Heron and Loon

the dream, then:

together we went, Indian style, thru the wet pine,
in search of the loon,

hand held lights diffusing
in the moonless fog.

together we moved,   and alone,   branches
brushing the sequence

of our silence, our
solitudes spaced between
the dim centers of
refracted light.

the loon.   the midnight madness:

who among us could have thought
at noon that we

at night could move
the loon to leave our
common refuge, here
where the river brings us
calm reflections of the sea.

who among us could have thought
that we possessed

the power of the moon, to draw
the tides of madness out,
to free us from the echo
of the sea

afterward,   the reality:

I had a dream once.   There was a great
blue bird, composed

on the bough of a pine.

'I could have touched–'

but distances are more
than dreams.   the loon
keeps his kind of distance
just beyond hearing
in the inner ear.
The great blue bird –
A heron, now I know –

is silent.

I could have touched him.

(fifteen years in the mind, the ear.   from maine to salmoncreek)

Echoes of Ourselves

Loons are lonely creatures.

        no

Loons sound like lonely creatures.

        no

Loons sound like ourselves
                   being lonely
       which is to say
            (I say)
     being
         (feeling)

     not whole—ly human.

There is Nothing to Do

there is nothing to do
            when the flower dies
                      and the pelican
   the shell
      (we used to say paperthin
              before we knew
              how thin that was)

     broken by the feathered weight
             of the nesting bird
   the rock

     stained to whiteness
            in seasons when shells
           burst with life
  and still

     (and can we still say 'still')
            and still the crash of waves
          welling up from the
         hint of history

    sounding the cry of the   onceborn

           listen.   let me tell you
   of a strange and beautiful bird

Birth Memories

The caul and the cord, breath withheld, a silent birth.

First memories are myth : memories of midwife and aunt
                Told to the mother   later   after the delayed cry

            Told to the child
                    over and over
                        (always eager, the child,
              to hear the myth
                  of birth,   the child
            forever the center and the onlooker
                  of her own beginning)

            Memories held by the child
                to be recalled
                    with each unwinding of the cord,
                    with each first breath.

The caul.   First shadow of the inward turning.

                  The midwife would not touch the blue child,
                        hooded in history;
                stood in the wooden light,
                shielding her eyes from
                    the infant's mystery.

              It was the aunt, always old in the myth
                and memory, who plunged
                  the breathless child
                  into the makeshift womb,

                  the shock of water that
            demanded breath
                    and being.

The memory of a memory becomes the myth : the stories grow and multiply.

Many mothers, many births.

And still, it is the same midwife,
　　　　　　　　helpless in the presence
　　　　　　　　　　　of the caul;

It is the same aunt,
　　　　　　　　Demeter surely, mother now;

It is the same child, unwinding the memories
　　　　　　　　　　of many births.

Cover Portrait

Robert Duncan/Bending the Bow

It is your left eye that turns.
The right looks straight ahead.

Do you see me in your periphery,
　　　　　your sinister angle of vision
　　　　　adjusting light to fill the shadowed form
　　　　　with colors of your own projection?

Or is it the right eye
　　　　　staring steadfastly into the center
　　　　　of your reflection, using my eye
　　　　　for a glass, that bears the childhood wound?

Glancing from left to right,
　　　　　I see the swift release of images
　　　　　and know
It is not your gaze which shifts.

The third eye bends the bow.

They Also Lie Down in the Sun

(a letter to my father)

The first time I saw
          cows in California,
I was comforted.

                    Ohio cows,
               as you had passed it down,
               reflected the weather.

          There was no doubt in your mind,
               nor mine, as I grew up,
               that cows always lie down
                              in the rain.

          A herd of cows   lying down
               on a sunny day–
          Well, it would rain before nightfall.
               And, of course, it did.

          It was one of life's predictables,
                    and I found myself
               testing it
                    in Pennsylvania,
                              New York, Maine.

          Look, I would say to the children
               in the car. The cows
               are lying down. It's
               going to rain.

          How do you know?

                    Magic. My father told me.

          Adults were not so awed. They
               wanted proof.

                    Never mind, I said.
                         You'll see.

So the first time I saw
            cows in California,
    I was grateful to see them
            standing stolidly
            in the clear September sun:

            it focused my
    childhood,
                        made
            the distance small.

It is only now

            since I have grown to know
            that
                        fathers, too, must
            become men.

It is only now that I can say
            to you

                        yes, it's going to rain.
                        the cows are lying down.

            But they also lie down in the sun.

For Robert Duncan and Sparrow
who Touched Him with Song

The dark boy spread his rug
                composed his body his song
                        cradled his harp
        and sang.

How do we describe the boy
                was he greek, persian, god
                        was his name orpheus, eros
                                ramachandra
        a pan in sheepskin   flowing madras
                strings tuned to the solitary note
                        of the lyre   sounding in time
                                through time
                strings of glass
                        stretched to the edge of breaking.
        The ancients had set for magic.
        We explain it away in advance and are caught
                        wordlessly
                in suspension of breath
                        when it penetrates
                        the closures of our minds
                stopping up our spirits in a
                        rush of aspirated
                        consonance, a hovering of
                OOOOOOOOOOOOOOOOOMMMMMMMMM

                        in the afterimage of the
                        small bird's song.
        The body of song may stretch the spell.
                (Who can play on strings of glass?)

Supposing that it's already been said, all of it.
                        What then.

What then of the moment we thought to hold in time with words.
What then of the song, the poet, and the boy.
What then of the sparrow, delicately balanced on strings of glass.

                Webbed words for winged thought
        Stay on the order of saying your body of song.

After the Memorial Day Dance

He told me (as if I hadn't
heard it before),
he told me about his leaving home
when still a boy:
the father's death when he was
very young,
the baby of the family, growing
into the incorrigible boy;
the cocky youth,
struggling to maintain
a position he had never really held,
yearning for the very love
he threw off in his young disdain
of all conventions, morals,
dull conservatism.

He never went back.
Once, to his mother's funeral,
but not to stay, or even to visit
with those he'd known before.
He was too proud to let them know
that he's turned out to be
the decent conservative sort that he is,
rather settled in his ways,
married to me.

for Selma

Eight O'Clock in the Morning
and it's Still Dark Outside

"Arriving at your classroom early will give you an opportunity
to see that your room and your lessons are in order for the day."

Every day it's the same thing – the room swept free
of yesterday's learning,
-the chairs
re formed in rows, and George Washington
still commander of the silence –

And then this kid appears, before the bell,
shoving his papered words
into the room in front of him.

I read the words, and it happens.

A rock, sculptured by the
sudden waterfall,
·   purples in the sun that is
rising over George's right
shoulder.

A small boy splays himself flat
on the tiled sand, molding
his bones into form, growing
fast into the reflections of himself
in the stream he gazed into
being.

A frog jumps, startling a new-blown butterfly,

An eagle's talons close.

Achilles pulls himself out of the river,
dangling his left foot, and
glancing at the boy's reflected beauty.

The kid is unaware of anything unusual.

He is sitting at the typewriter,
enthralled by the words deafening
the paper in front of him.

My room and lessons are ordered for the day.

Sometimes, on a day

sometimes
    on a day when everything
      (by which i mean not every thing
          but every one)

    seems to pile up inside
        your head and it is about to
          implode

sometimes
    on a day like that
      (by which I mean a day not
        'like' that or
        'like' today but
          today itself)

    somebody
        (or two or even three)
         takes hold of your eye
          with some words
            said out loud so
               gently

    everyone
        (who's listening)
         can hear and

    on days like that
        (like today)
         you know all there is
        to know

        about poetry.

For Alice

I'm sorry your bird is dead.
It won't help to say
Don't think about it or
Read a book or
Write a poem.
There aren't any magic words
For death in any form.
The size of death
Is relative, I suppose,
To the hole it leaves,
Not in the heart, as commonly
Supposed, but in the stomach,
Suddenly empty with a
Hunger not appeased by the
Neighbor's cakes and casseroles.
Nobody brings food for the
Death of a bird. It would be
Inappropriate. And
Nobody sends cards,
It's just as well.
To acknowledge the death
Of so slight a thing
As a bird
Seems presumptuous, somehow,
For such a private loss.
But I'm sorry he is dead.

Reply to My Fourth Period Humanities Class

Yes, I'll read you my poems.
Carefully selected? Of course.
I'll go over them tonight and
Weed out the ones that would
Break the mold, pierce the mask,
Reveal the other side of the
Janus you face every day.
Are you kidding?
Don't tell me you fall for that
Flagrant myth.
Don't you think I know
That the masks are off
The minute I step into this room?

Don't you think I know
That here in this room
Whatever face you ask for you get?
What do you think it means –
To be a teacher – anyway?
To wear a mask for eight hours
A day, or a different one for every class?
Oh, there are masks all right,
If you want to look at it that way,
But more than you suppose –
One for each of you, if you care to
Add it up. But they're all
Real. Yes, Real.
Do you suppose that any poem
I could write would tell you more
Than fifty minutes in this room?
If you happened to be
Paying attention?
Did you ever think about that phrase –
PAYING ATTENTION?
(you see I can't help teaching,
even now.)
You pay all right.
But what do you get?
Less than you pay for?
Sometimes.
        On an angry day.
On a day when the noise
Breaks my flexible sound barrier,
Or a day when the car refuses to stop
And takes me to Carmel
Before it comes back, empty,
In time for the perpetual bell.
On those days you get less than you pay for.
Do you ever get more?
And what do I get if I am
Paying attention to you?
I'll tell you what I get,
If I can
I get all that the two-faced
God got, standing in the same place
And seeing from two points of view.
I get to be seventeen, with a difference.
I get to be seventeen and twice seventeen
And all ages inbetween

At once.
I get to sit in a hard chair and
Be lulled by the drone of my own voice.
I get to write a poem every day
And read it new, for the first time,
Every morning.
I get to sit silently, never speaking,
Fearful of being called on,
Fearful of not being called on,
And I have to decide
Whether to call on myself.
I get to feel resentment at
Being called immature
When I feel like it.
I get to know the person sitting
Next to me, and I get to watch
The process of revealing myself
To another.
I get to stay home sometimes
When I'm not sick
Except of school
And wonder whether anybody
Notices I'm not there since I never
Say anything anyway –
And I get to take the roll
And notice.
I get to feel the frustrations
Of coming to school without my
Homework just because I didn't do it
Or because my mother was sick
Or my grandmother had died,
And I get to know the frustrations
Of having given an assignment
That I couldn't have done myself
And the unexpected joy in finding
It on my desk, scrawled or neatly typed
But every word perfect in its place.
And I get to pick a rose or a camellia
On my way to school
Just because it's there
And discover it later in the room
Unfolding its singleness
In a fire-tipped bloom.
And I get to know a few of you
And a few of my other selves through you

And watch the masks slip, slide, fall off,
Grow back, grow in –
All of them you
All of them myself,
All of them acknowledging the reality
That stands today unmasked in this room.

In Memory of Robert F. Kennedy

June 6, 1968   . . . First chill, then stupor, then the letting go.

Other people's words invade my own,
        . . . and I taste at the root of the tongue the unreal of what is real.

Fragments of phrases splinter in my skull,
            bury themselves in a sense – less attempt
            to re – form the day that splintered a life,
            a life time in a time of life.

Alterwise by owl light . . .
            I think continually of those
    . . . who traveled a short time toward the sun.

A moment in and out of time
                (Hurry up now, it's time
    . . . out of the cradle endlessly
                (when lilacs last.

Turning and turning
        . . . in and out of time's widening gyre.

The ceremony of innocence is drowned
        . . . in the mourning after death,
        . . . in the blood-loosed tide
                . . . of what is past or passing or to come.

His soul stretched tight
        . . . .its hour come round at last . . .
                . . . and left the vivid air.

Do not go gentle . . .
                (Humankind cannot bear . . .

Into that good night
                (the supreme fiction
                        flickering.   49

I do not Need to Know

I do not need to know the other side of death/
dying.
Teachers do not take the Hippocratic oath.

We have no snakes entwined
upon the staff of life.

The oath we take is silent/
sworn
to view
reality one way through
the looking glass.

(Present both sides. Take no stand.
Above all

do not influence your students.

Swear.)

And are there, then two sides to dying/
death?

The living know but one.

The raven screams my oath

stretching his wings
across the bloodied dove.

May 6, 1970
in response to the death of four students at Kent State

Brush Strokes

The Chinese artist knew
The brush to use, what tip
For the bamboo, what angle
For the wrinkled rock.
Their word, not mine,
The 'wrinkled' there with
Massive stone, evoking life
From cliffs that weather
Tides, grow fine lines etched
To hollows in the delicate brush
Of yesterday's many wrinkled moons.

Fire

Fire draws eyes, mind, ears
Into its promiscuous path.
Thought sucked into ash
Leaves charred mind
Smoldering at the black river's edge,
The fire-licked mind dying the death
Of self-consumed blaze,
Falling first to ember
Then to ash,
Which is not dead, you say,
But only changed

No wonder Heraclitus worshipped it.

Ash Wednesday

Wednesday drops its burning ash
Into the hope of forty days
Destined to be spent alone
In small Gethsemanes of our own.

The burning ash is quickly dropped
By one who thought to hold the flame.
The ash-red wound cannot be healed;
The Ash-red poem is unrevealed.

Ash to ashes without blaze.
Poem to words upon a page.
Features fade in view of face.
Words revolve in quest of grace.

Epiphany

There were other astrologers
    watching the heavens that night,
        other than the three.

They observed the star
    followed it far,
        with their eyes.

They stood, wise
    among men, saw
        it drop to rest

from where they were
    on the rise of a crest:
        it faded from view
        into the black-edged blue,
    and they noted the event
on their charts and placed

another star on their parchment
    scrolls, a cross there
        where it fell,

the strange blue star, witnessed
    far from the stable bed
        where the sudden star
        shed its inborn light.

There are other wise men
    watching the heavens tonight,
        other than the three
        who marked the first epiphany.

La Peine d'un Cheval

No harness, bit, or saddle
   binds this horse to his stolid pain.

Standing mute, stiff-legged
   by the somber spring of the tree,
   the fallen color of the sun,
  the horse bears his riderless anguish–

Bound by the harness, bit, and saddle
   of the brush that drew the artist's hand
   to draw this stroke of sadness,
   the wide black mark
   of this horse

  and this man.

Naming the New Dog

Old wine in new bottles –
Whichever way it was, Moses saw to it
That wine and the bottle both
Were old, and, befitting old,
Forever new.

The new dog comes to a place
Prepared, but not yet ready
To admit the old are gone.

The old names won't do. It's no use
Conjuring up old favorites.
He will be his own dog
With his own name
And his own haunts.

And yet
He will not be the same dog
He would have been
If the souls of the two great
Old ones
Were not looking on.

3/16/75   *Vasu 7-10-64 to 12-13-74*
For Vasu and Lark   *Lark 5-1-65 to 9-24-74*

Poem for an Afghan Hound

I want to write a poem for you
Vasudeva, old man of the river.
That's what your name means
Although you have never seen a river
or read the book that gave the name to you.
You know your name, though, and sometimes look
As if you're gazing into the river that joins
your life with his and sweeps them both
into the sea of myth and history.
You are a little of both, if you want to look at it
that way, the history less distinct than the myth,
and shallower. But the myth is strong and true.
You lived, old man of the river,
before time, when man and dog
hunted the shifting days together in the sands
and left no prints to tell to history
how one and one, not owned nor owning,
the man and you followed the sights and sounds
of life stretching before and after.

      Did you speak to the man then,
old man of the river, the way you speak to me
today – the elemental sounds that rise
out of the sandswept throat of the wind,
brushing my unknown thought with
hints of yesterday?
      Did you move then, old man of the river,
the way you move today when, loosed from the
civilized leash, you streak through the tall grasses,
with only the proud-ringed tail marking the
vanishing direction of your ecstasy?
      And did you sleep then, old man of the river,
stretched for warmth or comfort by the man
whose touch you rarely and disdainfully
permitted during the day, unless in gay
anticipation of the race or hunt you
playfully put on the antics of your young?

The myth moves into history, and time
gives shape and substance to the dream.
Speak, then, to the full-blown moon
of the shadowed night, run with primal
winds of the past, and in your restless
sleep, old man of the river, stretch full
to the length of history and let me share
the king-sized blanket of your myth.

Earthbound

The windowsill is filled with pots,
Red clay pots in old saucers, chipped bowls:
The spindly spider from the kitchen next door;
The avocado, sprouted after months of neglect,
Forgotten now by the child who learned at school
How to grow a tree; the coleus,
Paling in the long light.

I sit at the table scarcely aware
Of the space that they fill, guiltily remembering
The one need I know how to meet. After dinner
I will water them, being careful
To empty the saucers.

Rootbound, hungry,
The coleus turns toward the sun.

The Snake Can Grow only by Bursting its Skin

I can understand the solitude.
I can understand the search for the rock
That grows out of the earth leaving a
Dark hole, accessible only from underneath,
Open only to one with a bellycrawl,
A stretched skin
About to burst.

There is no molting without pain.
Skin is our only separation.
Skin is ourselves.
I breathe through my pores

To shed this skin I must flatten myself,
Crawl on my belly into the rock.
Let no light touch the painful crevices
Between the cracks on my skin.

What I do not understand is that we recognize
Each other when we emerge.
I have not missed you.
You have not missed me.
It is as if we had never been away

But I am different.
I have the new skin of a baby.

The Presence

This is no time for words. Not here
In the forest where I stand, shadowed
By madrone.

I close my eyes and
Spin myself a clearing.
The air is charged.

No one comes near.

(It was in such an atmosphere
the unicorn was born, linking
mind to memory and giving rise
to the intricate, embroidered myth)

There may never be a time for some words.
Not in the forest, not in the clearing.
Perhaps at the very edge of the held breath,
Where the mind dimly notes
The unicorn emerging from the shadow,
Perhaps then.

It is a gentle beast that enters here.

In the Threshold Sleep of Dark

In the threshold sleep of dark I reach
For where you never were, but are,
And come to you in China, yes, good night,
Until I dig my way from the dark of sleep
And weep into the wide awake of speech.

How Long a Ways to Never Land

(graffiti found on the wall of a ghetto school)
for Jeanette Sibley

Stone-scratched letters
        high up on the south side wall
                of the south side school
stone-scratched letters
        stretched to words
stone-etched words
        wrung from a voice
        dumb in the white
            face of ruled paper
        numb in the ruled
            face of—
                in the papered
            face of—
                in the silent voice of the
        hooded child—
                in the childhooded voice that
            touches the

space
                a stone's throw
        between the never
                never of the broken
                                land.

57

On Marking the Mind of a Student

Reading your paper   I am struck
    again
            (or still, for I am always
                reading your paper)
                                by the
        what can I call it
                                by the pure shaft
        of mind   splitting
                thought   into its known
                (but not to be proved)   smallest particles
reversing the assumption that
                                    fission
                is a disintegrating process.

Your words   set down upon the line
        (in ink, on one side only please,
            and watch the margins)
        shimmer randomly   and
                                    bounce
            against the whiteness
                            of the page
        there
                no
                    there
(How can I read them when they won't
                stand still)   indicating their presence only
            by their movement
                        by their
        ever-shifting dance
                        upon the lines
(now wavy to my eyes from trying
    to follow the optical illusions
                    of your mind).

Dance, logos, dance upon the page
        my red pen (felt-tipped, irrevocably)
                suspended
                            above you, not able
                to violate the poetry
                            of your prose
                descending only once
                                to inscribe
        in that signal, ineffective way
                    the mark of one mind
                            upon another.

Tony
(a haibun)

I carry the stone
heavy against my skin
crack--a geode!

It was the second week of class.
Things were just settling down.
The door opened.
Sudden silence as one more student—
there were no more chairs—
sauntered in
threw his change of program card on my desk.
Black shirt, black jeans.
Shiny black shoes with metal taps.
Heavy shades, as we called them then.
Tony
Tony Galena

My tenuous control of the class solidified.
Clearly they were uneasy,
aligned themselves with me.
Tony stood,
 refused to get a chair.
 Refused to get a book.
I couldn't see his eyes, but felt the
insolence from his posture,
the cocked head.

Days went by.
Tony came in late every day,
"Let me see your pass,"
He held it up.
"Let me see it," I repeated.
"You blind? Can't you see it?"
That was it. "Stay here after class."
After the bell, I was busy at my desk.
I had forgotten about Tony.

Suddenly aware of a presence behind me, I turned.
There he was, his back to me,
hand raised to touch an oil self-portrait
done by a former student.
I held my breath and watched as his fingers
slowly traced the line of the brush.
The room was empty.
"I kind of liked that poem about the crow," he said,
hand still raised in delicate tracery.

59

Love is Not to be Learned

Love is not to be learned all at once.
It comes over and over, a fresh skin
every time, the eyes deepening with
each suffusion, watching each new
face form

Poems are like that. New skins,
Fresh skins, bearing old loves
in wrinkled words and crow's feet
around the eyes.

Meditations on the Tarot: The High Priestess

I spread the cards on the kitchen table.
Three deep breaths. The mantra, silently.
Pick a card, Mother. Wait until
It feels right in your hand.

These are not the same cards
We deal out for euchre every night.
This is not the game that forces us,
Solitary, to make light talk, condensing
My three week visit
To a game of cards.

The one you pick will signify you,
Mother, set the stage for the reading.
Let your hand move across the cards.

Doctors never operate
On members of their families.
There are probes one should
Not make. Incisions
Requiring the steady hand
Of a stranger.

I move my eyes along the span of cards,
Following your hand. Two strangers.

Turn the card face up, here in the
Center of the table.

The High Priestess, Significator.

I should have known.
There is no other card in the deck
For you. It drew your hand
Once, twice, three times before
You picked it up, testing
Its strength, its draw.

High Priestess. Cosmic Mother.

Don't look so pleased with yourself.
You knew you would pick a power card.
I gather up the cards, place them
By my left hand, then one by one,
Form the Celtic cross and
Read the cards.

Power surrounds power
As the major arcana fall into place:
Below, the Moon,
Behind, the Star.
The reading flows.
Above, the Tower falls.

I hesitate, then,
Stranger to the woman sitting there,
Spell out destruction,
Change, and reach for
Death.

The card is there. I scan the
Woman's face. Serene.
She knew it all along.

There are no secrets in these cards.

Demeter: The Gift

The first time, she brought a gift.
Who is it, the hypnotist probed.
Ask her who she is.
No need, I know her well.
Core knowledge, bringing me seeds.

The garland of October fruit,
Brown and russet red,
Spills out, marking the ground.

At nine I held the fruit of Greece
In my hand, Libra, rising.
My fourth grade teacher understood.
She was, after all, responsible,
This early passion for the gods.

I watched the pomegranate grow dark
And leathery. It shriveled,
Sat on my desk, a dusky amulet.

But pomegranates grow only in Greece,
I shouted, running to the bush.
New home, new land, new love.
Pomegranates, weighting down the branches,
Pomegranates, splitting in the dry valley sun.

Demeter, knowing the time was ripe
Rewriting the myth. Let the seeds
Run red in her daughter's mouth.

Born in October.

Crow Crossings
Book III

Moving into Language

We walk
on the bones of our mother,
shape earth silence
into elegy,
mourn the lost words that
lie with her,
searching
for our own lost song.

In My Craft

after Dylan Thomas' "In My Craft..."

I am not driven, as Dylan was,
to die the greenlong days and
sing them into poetry. I do not
know how he saw those eyes, morning
into afternoon, rising beyond the
pale into words. Or how, singing
rage, he cast his grief into the
arms of all the grieving lovers,
old in dream and young enough
to weep into the waking of their
years. I do not know how Dylan
lived his sullen art. Nor do I
know how, silent and unannounced,
my quiet poems appear, pale
against those spewing words that
sing, once sung, inside my blood.
I know your music, Welshman,
carry the coals of those dark mines
in my hands. And yet, I do not rage.
I listen to the morning, in my
craft and quiet art.

Letter to a Friend in Vancouver

You   reach into my dream, see
the mating dance of the loons
(a chronicle, true to myth)

tell me you, too, were born in October
(the loon survives the sacrifice,
becomes phoenix, lives)

write clusters of words that fall
through time
forming layers of images
(forming and re-forming, loon to
phoenix, crow to raven to crow)

We talk here of technique. A man asks
can we teach it. I say
look at language.

Listen. There was the time in Grace Cathedral
I heard Pauline's music through
the soles of my feet.

There was the time I heard Nathan's
impeccably smooth violin, jagged
from the pulsing strobe.

You   write from a dream I had
before I met you of going to Vancouver,
to an island, of walking in concert
with crows, of listening to the land
through the soles of my feet.

The man speaks of teaching poetry. The poets.
They.

I want to talk about poems, I say. Us. Writing.
I want to write and read you my poem and talk
about how it is to begin again after a long time.

Your letter keeps falling out of my clipboard
where I carry it, like a talisman, meaning
to answer   but letting the days and weeks go by.

But tonight as we talk of poetry and technique,
I have something to say.   Suddenly
I understand design:

       In-spirit. In-corporate. In-form.

The earth approaches the equinox. Like you,
I move into the beginning of my year, spin
into the turning of the gyres.

Demeter prepares once again to search for her
daughter.

I keep my feet on the ground, hoping this year
to feel the point of balance between turns.

Artifacts of Poetry

I live inside a changing geometry.
Ratios are recast. Abstractions fall
to function. Elements, in frozen frames,
pinpoint particulars.

Yesterday, walking by the ocean, the sand
falling away underfoot, I sank into burrowed
space. My toes explored the empty home of crab,
clam, whatever lives in borrowed shells
filled with the trappings of lives
lived in succession. Inhabitants of shells, moving in,
filling drawers and walls, making our mark, moving on.

But what of the pens that cluster together
in the wolf mug on the desk, what of the
burgeoning bits and bytes of hard disk memory?
To bring these particles together
into form, to see the conjunctions, to make the
metaphor–to stop this dispersion
into meaningless bits and pieces–for this
we attempt, once again, to walk the loosely-
shifting sands, to probe for tracings,
proof of life, to realign the words.

Poem Hidden in Bamboo

I dip my brush into the black Sumi ink,
point it against the side of the palette,
hold it, poised, above the delicate rice paper,
then add one leaf to the bamboo.
Then another. Over and over,
the leaves give shape to the branch,
the trunk, which arches left to right, bends
in the breeze we do not see.

The effects are there, on the paper,
the wind known only by what it touches.
The bamboo grows in earth we do not see,
do not paint. The space defines what lies beyond,
the path through the village, into the cleft
between the mountains.

None of this is visible.
Only the bamboo
and a stroke designating the edge
of the snow cap on the mountain
we know is there.

Composition

The first thing I notice is the dog.
Then the statue of St. Francis.
Then the whole emerges—dog, saint,
church, pale adobe against the dark blue
of the sky. Still, the sun casts deep shadows
that impinge on the statue, throwing the stillness
of the dog into silent relief.

And so I myself am transported
to that scene, absent onlooker, knowing
that particular dog, those three crosses,
that embodiment of the saint, that sky—
each element that composes the whole—
only through the eye of the artist
who preserved in that moment the meaning
between one heartbeat
and the next.

for John LeBaron

Heron Standing with Cows

"On Lapis Lazuli: Mixed with lead white,
it maintains its purity even in the palest shades."
                    Jonathan Janson: Vermeer's Palette

The cows graze in the sun-flecked meadow,
immobile, placid: a lost Vermeer perhaps,
a landscape organizing light
shadowed by heavy violet clouds.

It takes a careful eye to see,
deep in the grasses, emerging
from the patchwork of black on white,
the statue masquerading as bird.

Wings folded, ruffled neck perpetually arched,
it poses as if waiting for the artist to mull
this precise shade of ultramarine, brush
the bird's crown with lapis, and paint this scene:

a great blue heron that chooses
the company of cows.

As I See It

Day by day, I write my world:
the bonsai crab apple blooms
again in October, unexpected
color in the shelter
of small trees. The walnuts
break out of their tough
green husks, ready for the crows
and ripe for our harvest.

In the back meadow, the young dog
stretches full out,
running free.
The old dog
runs a few steps after,
remembering.

The Persimmon and the Crow

When you have picked the last persimmon from the tree,
stand back. Look again.
Look until the leaves shift slightly in the breeze.
There, hidden in the burnished foliage that matches
the color of the persimmons in your bag, is the one you missed,
the one you will leave for the crow, who has already tasted
the ripe one that fell into your hand.
This one is, of course, perfect. As all things are that
reveal themselves only in that sudden slant
of turned leaf:
things that resist picking.

Icarian Bird

On Thursday, I witnessed a glorious thing, a golden bird swooping
through the garden, long arcs downward, then up with the
draft, flying far afield, into the orchard, then swooping
back into the apple tree outside the fence, branches
hanging above the Japanese garden. It didn't stop long,
just paused, then began arcing again into the sky. I had
never seen a free parakeet, for that is what it must have
been. I wondered where it had come from, how long it had
been free, whether it would be able to survive on its own.

Today I discovered its body lying next to the house near one of the
bonsai trees. There was no apparent injury, no unnatural
conformation. Just this beautiful golden bird with a
pattern of light green and pink on its sides lying still
under the small ginkgo tree.

And so now, I wonder: Was it freedom it was experiencing? Was it
fear? Was it searching for a way into the house, where it
thought its cage might be, waiting and open? Did it fly into
the window at dusk, when the golden rays of the sun were
slanting off its feathers reflecting the sky? Did it have
an Icarian moment of ecstasy flying into the sun before it fell?

Particularly the Redbud

Walking down an unknown street,
thinking about the path I took to get here,
I am startled: crimson blossoms
fall from ancient trunks.

Redbud, here!
The shower of petals transports me
halfway across the country to
thirty springs of redbud, dogwood,
yellow crocus in late snow.

This conjunction of disparates,
this discovery—all the redbuds:

preparation for this moment.

Why Does It Always Come to Poetry

Even in conversation, words
move to line, stanza, demand a title,
leave out great chunks of thought,
glide over sentence parts,

leave space for silence.

Expecting nothing back.
And everything.

I Am Always Learning Your Name, Over and Over

Some names stick. Like thistles
to socks, names cling to our walks
and we come home with a list of
identified flight, color, song.
The unnamed thing is staggering:
I squint my eyes against the sun,
trace wing bars, tail spread; count
the time it takes to fly out of my frame.

I have no name to
classify, sum up, discard the
throaty, slightly hysterical call
of the unfamiliar bird; no word for
the shade of blue, just this side of
sky, of that small flower that
clusters on the hill.

I am tempted to name the bird myself,
to give the flower a history. First
naming is poetry: the search for metaphor.
I will name the bird
and its cry will no longer
chill my bones.

The ancients knew better than to speak
the names of their gods. To know the name,
yet never speak the syllables, is to know
the heart of a thing, how it came to be
red instead of white, like the flowers
of the mulberry, stained with the blood
of the mythic lovers.

A lover's name is a secret thing.
To see in a flower the day's eye or
the tooth of a lion is to see it new
as I see you, undefined, unclassified,
your name to be learned, over
and over.

On the Fiftieth Anniversary
of Watching Meteors in Vermont

How is it
that once I saw your face,
I could imagine
no other.

Lying next to you on the grass
in the Vermont meadow
watching the meteors
flash silver across the sky
over the mountain

how could I know
I was destined to
live on the other side of
the country, transplanted
like the falling star
into permanence belied
by the fault-studded earth.

When You Leave

The compass shifts,
goes off its course. I spin,
dizzy without my bearings,
do not recognize the shape
of this house, this garden,
these hills that
lean in the direction
of cold suns as if to follow you.

The imagined light, extending
day into darkless night
makes sleep an anomaly of
some earlier time,
as if this moon I
write by could echo
the sun that has
spun this compass
off center.

Gradually, gaining my
balance, I walk the untoward
perimeters of this space,
say the name of each tree,
each flower. Inside, I rearrange
the walls, the paintings, stand
looking at the stove,
new and unfamiliar
without your eyes.

What are years, asks Marianne Moore.

I

Our lives are punctuated by anniversaries.
Today, my mother's birthday. A hundred and six.
Next week my father's. A hundred
eighteen. All those years. And here I am,
unable to comprehend this avalanche of years,
still a child, impervious to time.

II

They say aging is different today, that old age
has aged, that seventy today is what sixty was
yesterday. Or fifty. The years don't add up the way
they did. So why, looking into the mirror
early in the morning, do I see my mother's face,
pull the skin up by my eyes to watch the wrinkles
around the mouth smooth out, the way she did.
"See," she would say, "this is the way I used to look."

Old Man

Old man, bird weight,
I could hold you
in the palm of my hand,
feed you honey water
with an eye dropper and
put you into a nest
of old newspapers
by the door, hoping,
in the morning,
to find you gone.

How to Wake Up on Your First Morning Alone

First, ignore the barking dog as long as possible.
Then get up slowly so as not to erase
        your memory of my impression
        next to you.
Slip your feet into my Birkenstocks so your
        arches won't fall as mine did.
Walk quietly, because the dog is now silent,
        into the kitchen, out the sliding door,
        onto the deck.
Take the measure of the day:
        Temperature.
        Clarity.
        Sound. (You may hear the crow.)
Go back in and let the dogs up.
        They will run right past you, taking
        their own measure as they check out
        the smells of the day
        before they come back to greet you.
Lie down on the floor.
        Do your back and neck exercises.
        One dog will come over and kiss your face
        because your eyes are closed.
Sit up and face the sun.
Be quiet in this space.

Only then should you get up
and put on the coffee.
Only then will you remember
that you are alone–
you and the dogs,
the house,
and the day.

Touching Down

     I
Here among strangers,
knowing no one,
known by none, I sit
under seven madonnas,
write these last words.

     II
What is it we have not said?

     III
I reach over in my sleep.
Still there.

     IV
When I am not here,
who will make your coffee,
open the windows,
let the dogs up to
leap into your sleep?

When you are not here,
who will water your bonsai trees,
feed the birds, hand me my towel
as I step out of the
shower?

When we are not here,
who will stand on the deck and watch the moon
rise over the apple trees and the mountains,
marvel at the changing colors in the east,
notice the way the Bermuda grass is
taking over the front garden?

     V
In the next life,
will we recognize each other
as we did in this one?

It Was Grass, Not Flowers

It was grass, not flowers,
obsessed his later years, days
passed deep in the green
tending, calmed by the everydayness of the chores.
He came in like a farmhand
at noon: the cottage cheese,
the consommé–at the last
drunk, ritually, from the
crazed ironstone bowl. Then
back to the long expanse of afternoon,
no promise of bloom
enticing him to dig a patch
of grass for daffodil. No color
warranted his concern.

She stood at the kitchen window,
dishwater grown cold with memory.
She should have been prepared:
Once, when he was younger,
and preoccupied, she had planted
tulips, and chrysanthemums,
a long row beside the arbored walk.
It would be beautiful, she thought,
when they bloomed, and tended them.
But Sunday, returned from church,
she found him, sweat dripping
below the out-of-season straw,
white shirt sleeves rolled, no tie,
and the grass mowed and the tulips
sticking out of the great mound of
dead grass and
too, her eyes heavy,
even the chrysanthemums
(budded, never to open,
flame, flop, grow scraggly),
and now, tight and
glory hidden, she stood,
there at the window,
the grass
smooth and totally green.

Crystal Lies Implicit in the Sun

A letter to my brothers Dale, Don, and Bill: June, 1984:

Brother, I have never thought of you
dead. I think, I have thought, about
dying. Mother. Lover. Self. I have tried
to plan, to be ready. Willed myself
to know beyond. But today, thinking
of the four of us, quadrants of the earth
apart, I turned around and saw us
girdling the earth.

> Stay well, brother. Brother. And
> Brother.

Postscript for Don, who left this life July 17, 1994

In each life we awaken to so many uncertainties,
the time, the manner of the living and the leaving of it;
we experience anew the satisfactions, the frustrations,
know the hollowness of suffering,
the pervading spirit of love.

> Our soul-knowledge fades with each birthing
> and we are left to work our way through
> each life with approximations: intimations,
> the barest touch, the resonance of breath and voice:
> the heartbreak of a language
> that does not quite convey what we know.

> > The life you chose this time around
> > bore traces of many lives–
> > philosopher, poet, shaman–
> > lives you have led,
> > lives you will lead.
> > In the life you contemplate now, perhaps,
> > your dream of using language
> > to build a peaceful world
> > is already coming to fruition.

> > > Stay well, brother.

When the Earthquake Comes

My kitchen is cluttered with perishables—
baskets of lemons, onions, great purple heads
of garlic, oranges picked in the valley, apples
from our own orchard, a pineapple. The fresh bread,
dense and roughly grained, would last perhaps a week.
I have plenty of rice and lentils, but they need water
to cook; and my cupboard smells of coffee beans,
useless in an emergency.

I've been meaning to fill the water jugs
left over from the days of carrying water
to our ocean shed, but I haven't gotten to it
and they are collapsed in the garage beside the
dusty food dryer that ought to be on, day and
night, drying soups and stews, making jerky
for when the earthquake comes.

I have thought about what would fall
and said we should protect the Picasso vase
and his yellow-goated ceramic platter,
but they sit and hang, vulnerable as the
delicate, long-necked statue, "Mujer de la Rebosa,"
whom I have carried from house to house,
afraid to pick up, afraid to put down.
The slightest jar and she would crumble.

I can't believe the Pre-Columbian figure
would break. After all these years
in the earth, settling, it might perhaps
be buried again, and dug up, and placed
on someone else's handcarved, ancient chest.

How does one prepare
for loss? There is no insurance
for waking in the night
to find you, or me, or the earth
trembling.

Penelope, Weaving

"You can't keep weaving all day
And undoing it all through the night..."
"An Ancient Gesture" by Edna St. Vincent Millay

The words that formed patterns in the shawl,
the colors, so bright in the morning sun,
pale in the moonlight: violet becomes mauve,
yellow becomes amber,
the blue of the ocean outside my window
transmutes to an inky black, the surface
of the water still, empty.
What I thought I had woven into the fabric
is not there at all. The threads that were so tight,
the colors and ideas so precise, have fallen apart in my hands.

They think it is by design that I weave all day
and unweave by night, but the truth is, the
unweaving is not of my doing. It happens as my hands
attempt to read what I have woven and discover
that what I thought I had said,
the shawl I thought I was weaving
is only fragments of thread,
strands of half-formed words, complete
only in my dreams.

And still, in the morning, I will look out at the ocean,
now reflecting the blue of the sky,
and at the sun, gold as the chain I wear
around my neck, and my hands will once again
take up the threads, winding new spools,
throwing new shuttles, weaving.

Sunday Breakfast at Willow Wood

"I suppose you'll have the usual, right?"

"Right. The French Folded Eggs and a triple shot latté."

But when they came, all I saw was the golden mustard that had popped out overnight in the meadow, in the apple orchard, in the vineyard between the rows of dormant vines—mustard, everywhere, the color of French Folded Eggs which lie on my plate in their mustard perfection surrounded by the bare branches of hundred-year-old apple trees. And the way the sun pushed away the clouds and let the rain remain on the branches hit the yellow mustard in a brazen reflection of itself, and it was as if the sun had settled into the earth and come up beaming.

I looked down into my plate of French mustard eggs folded into a perfect breakfast. The latté was dark and hot.

On the Origin of Ritual

> The Hughes Aircraft laboratory in California has
> developed a "tilt meter" so sensitive that it has
> been able to record lunar tides in a cup of tea.
> Lyall Watson in Supernature

The moon turns. I pause, cup in hand.
The level drops and landlocked tide runs red.
As seaweed etches patterns in the sand,
the teacup tips to contemplate the dead.
I read the drying leaves the leavings left:
The ocean drained denies the moon its pull.
Fortune follows lines. The palm's bereft,
the tables turn and Tarot turns the Fool.
Years spin into hours, collapse in time.
The wafered moon, loosed from its earthly trance,
spirals, flashing holograms of rhyme
and poets match the dark side of the dance.
The ocean steeps in kettles brewing tea;
a drop of water comprehends the sea.

Reflections on Finding Algae in my Hair

Floating in seaweed fine as lace,
fingers drifting delicate tendrils,
we talk salt-water words.

So this is Florida, I say. The panhandle.
What I know of geography
is the lay of the land from 33,000 feet
in the air. But floating here, I am
in Florida. And know it.

The sun throws crepe paper
banners across the sky. I speak
cerise. You answer pink, reflecting
the cast of my mind on the water.
I know what you mean, I say, not sure
whether it is your words or mine
I have just heard. I think, in these
filaments of philosophy, I have
known this spit of sand before.
It is not chance that I, far from
my earthquake country, am here, floating
in this eye of hurricane.

The earth obligingly shifts. Awkwardly,
suddenly shallow, we readjust our
centers and, on tentative, newborn legs,
walk out of the water,
dripping green and laughing
like mermaids.

After the Stroke

for Selma

Can you paint the silence, I ask finally,
placing the canvas before her,
the brush in her left hand,
not the right, which lies inert by her side.
She doesn't look at the canvas.
The brush falls to her lap.
I move her chair closer to the table,
arrange the bottles of inks within her reach.

Her eyes move to the walls. Someone has
brought her paintings here, covered the
green, institutional walls with the vivid golds,
blues and purples of her abstractions.
They hold her gaze and mine.

The silence, I say again.
Show me.

Ignoring the brush, she grasps the bottle of
cobalt blue, steadies her eye, begins to
pour it on the canvas, a wide, sweeping arc.
Then gold, familiar, green where it puddles into blue.
One by one, she adds a drop of red, a line of
purple, then reaches again for the blue.

Spent, she leans back in the chair, looks
at the canvas covered with running lines
and pools of color, then, haltingly,
reaches forward, picks up the last full bottle,
and drowns the canvas. Black.

On First Hearing Carolyn Kizer Read Her Poems

All day the poets came to the big auditorium, read their poems, and left.
The audience came and went, too, depending on the name of the poet.
The big names, of course, drew the big crowds, English teachers
in and out of the room between workshops, luncheons, speakers.
Some few of us eschewed the workshops and stayed. On and on and on.
Poet after poet, poem after poem, until they began to run together,
the poets and the poems, and still we stayed, listening, waiting,
waiting as if for something to happen.

And then, striding onto the stage, her long hair free and golden,
her movements fluid and graceful, a poet I did not know, had not read.
She reached the podium, looked out over the room, arranged her features
into the wry smile I have since come to recognize,
and began to read.

Suddenly I was alone in that huge space.
There were no rustling programs,
no jostling in the rows as people came and went.
I might as well have been in a planetarium, the room darkened to focus
the ear on the measured rhythms, the pinpricks of sound
that slowly emerged into constellations of words:
the great bear, the hunter, the seven sisters.
"From Sappho to myself, consider the fate of women," she said.
And then considered it.

Nearly forty years have passed since that marathon reading in Houston.
And still, even though I have heard her read many times since,
have been included in small dinner gatherings in her honor
at the home of a mutual friend, have read most of her work,
have used her poems in poetry classes and workshops around the country,
have included her poems in books I have written for other teachers,
still I remember the electricity of that first reading,
the charged moment when I realized , at last,
something did happen in that auditorium that afternoon.
What happened was Carolyn Kizer.
What happened was poetry.

Things I Will Never Do in this Lifetime

I'll never live in an adobe house in New Mexico,
walls two feet thick, recesses built into unexpected surfaces,
Navajo rugs on the floors, walls, sculptures in red clay,
an O'Keefe hanging in the bedroom,
ochre and umber washes coloring the kitchen,
redolent with hanging red chilis, purple garlic, onions . . .

I'll never live by the ocean in a redwood house,
angles slanting toward the sea, inside glass and stone
and the crash of waves predictable as the moon, punctuating
the pattern of my days . . .

I'll never live in the house of the artist I'll never be,
a memory wherever my eyes alight, color cascading
in fabrics from Morocco, Turkey, Afghanistan, paintings
bold and vibrant, sculptures of women standing, sitting, encircling space,
randomness overlaid by a deep sense of structure . . .

I'll never know the source of my draw to Egypt,
studying the ancient texts, knowing the feel of the earth
when the waters of the Nile recede.

I'll never know the origin of certain memories–
the cloistered life in Normandy,
tending sheep on the hills in Spain,
trekking with my wolfdogs in the frozen tundra,
painting frescoes in the caves of Cappadoccia,
waking in the white hot buildings of ancient Greece,
vestal virgin to Helios, slave to priests, holding the
great sacrificial birds.

I'll never conduct a Mahler symphony or sing the role of Mimi
in Bohème, never again read Wallace Stevens all the way through
sitting on a small bed in Vermont, never read Finnegan's Wake . . .

I'll never spend an entire day in complete silence,
unencumbered by the need for food, for print, for voice.

I'll never live in perfect simplicity:
one table, one vase, one chrysanthemum,
one book of haiku.

Clarity

"The ground before my doorway must be telling me something."
Dave Hopes

Not only the ground but the sky, the sky. Filled with swallows claiming
the birdhouses one by one. (What must it look like inside those wooden
houses scattered around the edges of the orchard are there eggs yet or
perhaps baby birds?) Beyond the bird houses, beyond the ancient apple
trees jagged from the branches fallen deep in the grasses not yet mown
providing cover for the deer oh the deer that leapt across the driveway
on my way to get the mail and almost disappeared into the grasses but
stopped, turned, and stared at me all the way down the road and when I
walked back up to the house, there it was, still standing, still staring, and
the dogs on the deck staring back, not barking, but beyond the grasses
and the deer there is over the mountains a veritable–how to describe
the color–a vibrant sunset that surrounds this house, this land, this bird
space, this deer space, a sunset in the north, in the east, and south, too,
and then I have to go into the house and climb up the spiral staircase to
the only place where I can see all the way to the west, practically to the
ocean, and yes, the sunset is there where it is supposed to be, but not as
bold, not as purple, not as red as in the east. I don't have any words for
the colors that deepen and change as I look now for the deer but see the
only the birds beginning to settle into the approach of darkness, and the
sky, yes, the sky is telling me something.

Everything startles in its transcendence...the ancient trees, contorted,
hollow-trunked, stark against the new-meadow green, the white prints
of the raccoon that traverse the newly painted fence top leading to the
bird feeder, the seven crows strategically balanced on bare branches.

Oh the clarity, if even for just this moment
when we, like the crows, are still, waiting.

Fragility

More and more frequently, I am reminded of the fragility of our lives, of our loves, of what we have built as our way of life. We expect it to go on forever, even as we know it will not. These are clichés, yet those of us who find our bedrock in language, say it again, over and over. We say it one way. We say it another. We might find we have written a poem about apple trees that bloom past their bearing, but it is the same thing we have said before. We might find, as I did in a sequence of coincidences, unlikely reconnections, one starting with a poem posted by a person on my favorite online list of writers. The poem began, "The ground before my doorway must be telling me something." I loved that line and immediately used it to begin a poem of my own. Of course I then had to send my poem to the original writer, whom I did not know as he had not posted before to that group. We connected through Facebook and I then, checking out his list of friends, came upon the name and photo of a poet I had known very well some thirty-five years ago. She was a free spirit, constrained in a classroom. We exchanged poems and dreams and she set off for Greece. All these years I have known that someday we would reconnect. And there she was, a friend of a poet I had just met online. She had gone to Greece, bought a castle remnant on the island of Kythera, wrote another book of poems, and came back to her family home in North Carolina. And now, free spirit still, she is setting off again for her Greek island home. How to explain these convergences in our lives? Just last week, another connection, the name of a friend from long ago, one with whom I shared a summer in the early days of the U. C. Berkeley Writing Project, 1974. We have seen each other occasionally over the years, at a conference here or there. He lives and teaches in Louisiana. But now, on his birthday, his name comes up on my Facebook page. It has never been there before. We have not spoken or corresponded in many years. Surprised, I read the birthday messages from his many friends, but they are messages of sorrow. I write, to ask. He responds: his wife, his Sarah, whom he has loved for 43 years, is dying. Will die today, he writes, or tomorrow. It was a sudden, virulent cancer that settled in her spine. Such a gentle man. He says he can't stop crying. I cry for him, for his Sarah, for my friends, my partner, my self. For all of us. We have friends, we grow apart, we scatter across the country, across the world. We end up on mythical islands, the connections tenuous or buried under the everydayness of our lives.

The years pass. We change. We gain weight. We lose weight. The seasons remind us of small things. The swallows come in May, leave in August. The dogs grow older before our eyes. I write into silence. Sometimes a miracle returns. The globe is round. It has no ends. We spin into space. We are dizzy with memory. We are ill. We recover. Some time it will not be so. But now we are well. We love each other. We love this life. It is a fragile gift.

The Untoward Crow

The untoward crow
sits motionless on the
bleached bones of the dead tree—
a still life posed, waiting.

What tremor in the earth or air
would prod that bird to
    shift its weight
    unfold its wings
    announce its demarcation
        from the tree? from me?

Sound and Silence

Moving out of silence
Out of the white space –
  the distance between words
  the distance between languages
  the distance between us –
Into that silence, a word spoken
In that silence, a word heard

How is it heard?
How does your hearing
change my utterance?
How does my listening
allow your word to enter
  the silence?

Word by word
the poem is spoken, is heard
  changes the silence
  charges the silence
    with sound.

The Consciousness of Stone
Book IV

After the Fire the Stones

For Odin,
the Great Pyrenees
guard dog
and his goats,
the stone-swept
meadow was the place
of survival when all around
there was no barn or
shelter, just the flat
oasis of stones
in the midst
of
destruction.

Stones do not burn.
They remain in place
silent holders
of secrets
known only to the preservers
of words spoken
into the flames
centuries of codified
silence
in stone walls, houses,
fences, flat patches
in
fields.

Grace Precipitate

Cut to the fool. Discard the illusory cups.

On the precipice, the fool stands,
oblivious of the shaled rock
edging into space.
The dog leaps at her feet,
ready to follow her
anywhere at all.

It is grace that saves her.

The rose, delicately held in the left hand
(But it was a day lily that marked our walk
together, gave rise to poems, letters)

The rod, the walking stick balanced on the right
shoulder, diviner's rod
(But who could have told us, there in
those gentle mountains, of the days that were
to bring us to these cliffs.)

The magician's tools slung in a pack—cups, swords, wands, stars
(But how slow I was to learn the chaliced way,
hone the bladed intellect, pick up the
witching wand, put by the pentacle.)

The sun fills the corner of the card,
touches, does not melt, the ice-peaked mountains
clearly defined in yellow sky.

The fool, numberless, steps into
life.

Shuffle the cards. Cut. Shuffle. Cut.

On the precipice, the fool.

Grace Immutable

the same walls
with the same paintings
the cow still visible in the field
Turkish rugs translate the floors
into familiarity

everywhere in these houses
books read, unread
Plato, Frost, Stevens
books sedate, scattered
tables, shelves, floor

the ancient chest
16th Century Florence
once again and always
the place holder for Picasso's vision
now, your photo and urn

our houses fold into one another
large pool in one
small pool in another
hot tubs on decks, in greenhouses
bonsai clustered in shelters

the dogs run freely in the meadow
up the hill, on decks
each one unique
each one exactly like the others
couches full of dogs

kitchens look out on acres
of apple blossoms
cascades of azaleas, rhododendrons,
hillsides of fences bordering daffodils
redwoods up the unpaved road

trees leave and return
redwoods, apples, eucalyptus,
poplar, persimmon,
lemon, walnut--and the birds
always the birds

in the Japanese garden
or on the deck the stone
Buddha reminds us of
the constancy of change

Grace Ascendant: The Final Grace

At the moment of your death I too was transformed.
I live with a knowledge new to me.
I live with the knowledge of all the people I love and have loved.
I live knowing the transformative power of love.
Of those loves. Of those people.

I am a different person living a different life,
living it with you in a more complete way.
Nothing impinges on this belief
which gives me freedom to be who I am,
who we are, with one heart.
　　　　Without reservation.

I now understand the fine discriminations of love
　　　　carried in the language of ancient Greece.
I understand the value of Agape.
I understand Philia, which allows me to carry on my work.
And most treasured of all, Eros, the sensually based love we lived
even unto and beyond the moment of your death:
Eros, the love that aspires to the non-corporeal,
　　　　spiritual plane of existence and,
finding its truth, experiences transcendence.
I live now in a state of oneness I had not imagined before you left.
In a state of Grace. The final Grace.
　　　　Grace Ascendant.

Heaven's Wing
a Ghazal

It was the buzzard that got my attention,
Lying there, all intention lost to sky.

Thinking of nothing else, neither buzzard nor I,
Wings of angels thrust broken into the bleak black sky,

All intention lost in obsidian silence--
Angels and buzzard united in star-studded stillness.

Then I, focused on intention, buried my eye,
Seeing deep into the aching loss, while that black bird

Of Heaven, charged with the cleansing of the soul,
Gave up its dark duties of the visceral night,

Lost to sleep, lost to the waking tension
Of the day, lost Oh Buzzard, to Heaven's wing.

The Seventh Fear

Here on this holy ground
sanctified by your presence
>   the music of the spheres
>   awakens me, but
>   the shadow in Plato's cave
>   gives me voice

I wake to the sound of the stream
>   of no language
>   and look to the stars
>   of no speech

Rescued from depravity
>   dog falls to salvation
>   and learns the power
>   of happiness without fear
When the sun chose to rise
>   dog gave up the bone
>   of fear (as did I)
>   and the seventh fear
>   retreated to shadow

Speak to me of languages
>   lost to the stars
>   swallowed by black holes
>   spoken only in the shadow
>   of the moon struggling to rise
>   stark against the mountain
>   (that obsidian obelisk hiding the sun).
dog   freed from silence
speaks in sounds
>   behind the tongue
>   in sentences too ancient
>   to be understood

Breath after Breath

Moving through water
one arm after the other
alone in this primal world

one with the rhythm of the river
of the sea of the pulsing
womb of life

here where there is no sound
save the blood pulsing
in my body in my ears

marking every stroke
with intention with internal
knowledge not found in words

but known by the continual
wash of water this rhythmic
testimony to life

one with the sweet song
of the whale that courses far below
in a world I can only imagine

in those moments when I
hold my breath and lower
my whole body into that realm

where I no longer need
the intake of air to glide
smoothly replenished

by that momentary sense
of another world
then, rising effortlessly

back into the rhythm
of breath after breath of air
warmed by the sun

Final Eclipse

I

That first eclipse
shuttered the sun
its colors purpled
the skydark air
stars trembled
and the people
stood still

II

when the sun
disappeared
during the hunt
the mastodon
found refuge
in the wide open
space

the people watched
the mountain
fall into the water
as the penumbra
darkened the plain
between the shadow
of the moon
and the hidden sun

birds searching
for their nests
swept the sky
in great scarves
of ravened geometry
and the people
covered their eyes

III

eons later
what does it matter
to know that exotic particles
operate against the wishes
of gravity
when you see
the world
you have lived in
all these years
darken
before your eyes

you scan
the sky for birds
but they have all
flown toward the moon

and you know
you are
completely
inextricably
alone

Writer's Block
for Les

I know the shadow
of a poem
keeps you from writing

but shadows are full
of language
shrouded in mystery

and it is the mystery
you seek
always the shadowed

slanted, obscured view
of life
among the solitary

but when you feel
the music
of dissonance

is too much to bear
as the sun
shines on your reality

and you know
how temporary
the seasons of life are

you retreat to the cave
Plato engineered
to escape the poem

With This You

Wilbur is right, to rescue ideas with poetry.
Abstractions do not live without the persons,
the places, the things. Perhaps we ourselves
are abstractions. Perhaps we rescue ourselves
by creating places we have made our own,
leaving a trail of fences, moving the Picasso,
the fragile sculpture Mujer del Reboso, and the bags
filled with stones from our retreat at the ocean.

Losing touch with these realities,
I withdraw, disappear into the imprecise,
the vague, the general. It takes the other, then,
to rescue self, ground the scattered light,
focus illumination here in this last place,
with these things, with this you.

On Taking the Measure of Your Book
for Michael Franco

there must be a way
to enter your poetry
the way your words turn
into meaning after meaning
into the depths of memory
into the silence of the beach
which of course is never silent
but it seems so when I am there alone
and then the birds come
over the dunes
the tiny sandpipers,
silent in sand
creating the rhythm
of your poem
and far out beyond my eyes
the great white pelicans
and as I watch them I see
how I must enter your poetry
wings folded against the wind
as I slice again and again
into the measure of your ocean
there where silence is translated
into language

Litany

For all that is done and said.
We know their dream; enough
to know they are dreamed and are dead.
from Yeats' "Easter, 1916"

Enough to know.
They are dreamed.
And are dead.
The litany in my head
utters their names
one by one.
Dead. Not dead.
Dreamed.
The beginning. Kneel down
on the cold stone floor
of my dreams.
The stone of the heart recalls first
the great-grandmother's name:
Flora, from the isle of Tiree,
who brought with her to Ohio,
knowledge of Latin and Greek,
and the words of Shakespeare.
Far from the Scottish Hebrides
Flora's son Donald, and Mary,
his young bride from Wales,
started their family
and Mary gave birth
to Marietta Walker,
first of their twelve children.
Then Donald, their son named
after his father.
Then Carrie. Bill. Sam. Norval.
The family grew, boys
following their father
Into the coal-dark days.
The girls stayed in school
like their grandmother from Tiree.
They lost a child, Kenneth,
dead from typhoid.

Then came Maggie May,
the middle child,
(Maggie May, Margaret, Midge—
All names worn by my mother.)
followed by Mary Elizabeth (Betty).
Elbert. Lucy Florence.
and the youngest, Robert.
Twelve children
and never an angry word
in that household.
The names go on,
but my knees,
on that ancient stone
known only to memory,
have no feeling.
Only telling.
The names
come faster.
They are harder to say.
The brothers.
Dale, Don, Bill.
The cousins.
Their children
and their children
And now, in silence,
the stone.
My heart.
My love.
Say it.
Enough to know.
Dreamed.
And dead.

I Took Her Name

I never thought to change my name.
Born knowing it was women I loved,
we did not have the custom reserved
for others. Marriage was not a possibility
even though we lived together,
worked together, shared everything—
dreams, clothes, dogs, bed.

After fifty four years,
during which life changed
around us, laws that had seemed
written in stone, opened up
new ways of thinking about our lives.
We married, thinking it was for the cause
but found it was really for us.

Still, we never thought to change
our names. Until…
until, not the way we planned it,
(we were to be together, somehow)
she was gone. I alone remained
living for both of us, and I wrote a poem,
signed it as usual, then, almost without
thinking, added the hyphen
and her name became mine:

                    Fran Claggett-Holland

My Father on the Page

Once, out of the blue, my father,
my serious father, not given to excess,
not given to hyperbole, or metaphor,
said: I always thought I would grow up
to be a poet. No elaboration. No mention
of reading poetry in his youth.
Just that.

Years later, reading Wallace Stevens
for the first time, the entire opus
at one sitting, turning page after page
sitting on a small cot in our cottage
at Bread Loaf, in Vermont,
I remembered that moment.
My father a poet? What would it have
been like? What might he have written?

And now, rereading those poems
I know almost by heart,
I know why I was reading
Wallace Stevens, poem after poem,
hardly breathing between them,
knowing I was breathing them into my being,
into my brain, into my heart,
knowing for the first time in my life
my father on the page.

It Makes So Little Difference

It makes so little difference, at so much more
Than seventy, where one looks, one has been there before.
                                        Wallace Stevens

At so much more than seventy,
The given allotment. At seventy I will fly,
my father said, but he did not.
He had been flying all his life
driving out to the airport Sunday afternoons
to watch the planes, those magnificent birds
that could take him up up and away but did not.
He did not fly.

At so much more than even eighty,
I speak now for myself. Of course I have flown
many times, but Wallace Stevens,
as always, has it right. Where one looks,
where one flies, one has been before.
Where one has gone in poem after poem,
never mind the travel to Turkey, to China,
never mind those Egyptian hieroglyphs
speaking my name, never mind that my hounds
stared back from the sarcophagus of this
or that Ramses, I have been there before.

And I will write it again. And again.
I have flown with Icarus and fallen
into the Icarian Sea. I have been ravished
by Zeus. I have traveled into the underworld
to rescue my daughter and there, I have tasted
the seeds of the pomegranate and become
Persephone. It all began when I was a child
and my world opened into myth and I fell
in love with Augustus, who became my father.

But it was Sappho with her fragmentary lines
who determined my fate. Sappho who became
my muse, my love, the one who held my pen
and wrote into the heart of life, into the heart
of my love, into love itself. It is and was Sappho,
who rescued me from the temple where I had been
the vestal virgin of the sungod Helios, long before Apollo,
handmaiden to the priests, forced to hold those
glorious birds above the marble altar where the priests
gutted their innards to read the future of their fated
city, where the priests violated the purity of the
birds and of the girls who had been ordained to serve
their black-frocked selves, yes it was Sappho who
rescued me from that life and gave me another,
a life of love that has lasted me until this day,
these many lives later.

And now we write. We write about the particulars:
we write about the way the apple trees blossom
on dead branches. We write about the way the raven
casts its spell on every spit of land or home
we have called our own. We write about the hounds
that have followed us across the desert with Alexander
and found their way into our lives, conveying in
language only we understand, the tapestry of all
we have known before.

It makes so little difference, we who are earthbound,
we write to fly and continue to write, knowing
we have written it all before.
All.

Tanka

raven-winged Icarus
flies into the sun
defies myth
lives to cast his eye
into my heart

■

below five Chinese cows
bronze cave horse
searches for grass—
oh Matriarch of Eohippus,
the keyaki chest is barren

Nayarit man sits
with empty jars—
grass, cows, horse, man
I am humbled
by opulence

■

outside my window
the early flowering plum
blossoms pink silence
ancient philosopher Chuang
drums and sings to his dead wife

lifting my eyes
from your letter about Chuang
suddenly a breeze
snow blossoms sweep through the air
drumming my petaled heartsong

■

cows cluster
under live oak trees
It is enough
the nearness
of each other

after the first rain
the hills are
achingly green
I shut my eyes
acutely alone

waves of quiet
weariness sweep through
the redwood trees
I sigh into their
immovable weight

■

behind the flaming
colors of fall
some trees maintain
their August
green

■

now that leaves
obscure the branches
you, too, are hidden
and I am left
with only your voice

mockingbird
sings in runes
no spaces
between the notes
your song

■

missing the birds
a purple finch
flew in
filling this dark heart
with color and song

∎

6:42 a.m.
morning comes late
the redwoods stand mute
no birds so early
only my eyes to note the silence
of the sun-tinged sky

7:32 a.m.
trees suddenly green
in slate colored sky
the promised warmth
of the day disappears
into the invisible sun

7:59 a.m
and then!
crow alights
in the top of the unleafed tree
and sun bursts forth singing
its arrogant song

∎

Oh, empty ledge
where once you landed
so briefly
my heart remembers
the beat of your wings

∎

two hidden voices
one high and keening
the other low and shrill
I scanned the trees   '
seeking

seeking
the elusive crows
suddenly
the sun blazed evening
cawing between the trees

■

seven crows
circle in the snow
each flake unique
a carmine border
my coffee mug

■

Late
in her writing life
she experimented
with punctuation
especially the period.

■

because
you wrote the poem
the one
that is the painting
of K'un mountain

■

be present
    let your eye rest where it will
    consider the fulcrum
    leave room for dreaming
    surprise yourself and your reader

■

on Occidental Road
fields of mustard echo the sun
suddenly
here in this car on this day
unknown and alone

■

three redwoods
untouched by moon
or season . . .
my sense of permanence
in this changing landscape

■

the long table
set with elegant
simplicity
brought your family
into perfect harmony

■

Another Night, Another Porch

Eighty-two years ago, a child, alone on the porch,
sitting, staring at the sky, seeing for the first time
the stars suddenly encompassing
"what all of us will be swept into,"
seeing, as she sat staring into the sky alight
with patterns that explained the night, the voices
just beyond the window, the people talking
in a language she had never heard, glimpsing
through the window the long shape of a wooden box,
seeing dimly the face of her grandfather sleeping there,
knowing as she had never known before how she was
part of everything that she had ever witnessed
in all the lives she had ever lived, and knowing
her grandfather would hold her on his lap
and let her tell him about it in the morning.

NeonAura Starlite Divinity

For NeonAura Starlite Divinity,
the night that the star Regulus conjoined with the full moon
and received the beautiful Diva into Sirius

Full Moon Empty

Tonight the wolf moon.
Tonight the Diva moon.
Tonight the moon that will tell all,
Will probe the fine nerves that run
From the heart to the feet,
The feet that turn under, camel feet,
Not supporting the body that
Strains to stand, to walk, to howl
At that full moon rising purple over the
Mountains, etched against the sky.

Tonight, beloved Diva, sleep.
Sleep, Saluki, sleep.

Wicca

Afghan Hound Ch. Cavu's Wicca of Ghamal

How can you write about
the death of a dog, they say,
when there is so much human suffering.
I don't answer.
I know about human
suffering. I read the paper,
watch the news.
People I know are
dying, I don't deny the
pain, the human suffering.

But driving alone
down University Avenue
my eyes start with tears
and it is the Saturday in December
before Christmas
and I go inside--
Animal Clinic, Intensive Care--
and she is lying there
on her side, panting,
the tubes running in clear,
running out pink
with blood that should have been contained.

The thing is, you can't write
about your dog dying, her tail thumping once
even then as life dripped away.

At home, Holden, her coltish son,
lastborn, no longer looks for her.
He jumps up, feet on shoulders,
nibbles my chin and looks at me:

her eyes, her eyes.

Making Room for the Other

a poem for BodhiMitzvah

When the old dog crossed the rainbow bridge
and the young one was left alone,
something magic happened.

All those comments about how the young one
wasn't as smart, didn't learn as fast,
would never be as clever, as beautiful, all true.

For so many years, there was no comparison.
There was only the One. She ruled.
She was the perfect pet. And she truly was.

Nobody would say otherwise,
Especially the young one, new to her people,
her new world, no clue as to how to be

Appropriate. Not on her couch. Oh no.
And she never played. She didn't know how.
She had never had a toy of her own.

Or a person. And now she had two.
Two to please. Whatever that meant.
So she did the best she could.

And one day she found out she could
Snuggle up on the couch. Just like the old one
Used to, even though she had her own bed.

And she found her person was always there.
And her person's person was there, too,
Looking at her with new eyes.

Eyes that said, we will never give you away.
We will never let anyone hurt you.
We will always love you.

You are beautiful. You are smart.
You are not the old one, whom we will always
Love. But you are ours and you love us

And we will take care of you.
And love you just for who you are:
Learning to be our dog.

Attributions

Front cover painting: "Heroic Crow"
Pat Cheal ©2021
oil on panel, 18" x 24"
www.pattheartist.com

Back cover painting: "Raven's Dream"
Eric G. Thompson ©2021
egg tempura, 24" x 19"

Dedication: "The Journey of the Ladybug "
was inspired by Patricia Fargnoli's poem
"The Last Day" from her award-winning Duties of the Spirit.

From: "This Consciousness that is Aware"
Title is from Emily Dickinson's poem #822
Italicized words in I are from Robert Duncan's
"Food for Fire, Food for Thought"
Earth artist referred to in II is Michael Heizer

The phrase "certain slant of light" in
"On the Eve of Autumn"
is from Emily Dickinson's poem #320.

"The Predicament of Being Human"
is in response to a Warren Bellows painting.

The poem "Just Human After All" was written in response to
the "monster poems" of Patricia Nelson.

Michael Franco, who wrote the Afterword, is an author, poet, founder of Xit, Poetry Readings and Art Exhibits, fine letterpress editions with hand-drawn illustrations, Somerville, Massachusetts. The poem "On Taking the Measure of Your Book (for Michael Franco)" was printed in the New York Times Magazine October 4, 2020.

Freeman Ng, who wrote the Forward, is an author, poet, digital artist, and software developer. His latest work is Basho's Haiku Journeys, with illustrations by Cassandra Rockwood Ghanem. He also has written Joan, a Young Adult retelling of the life of Joan of Arc, and Who Am I, a personalizable children's book with 20 versions. In addition, he worked with Peter Scott Dale to write Poetry and Terror, Politics and Poetics in Coming to Jakarta.

About the Author

Fran Claggett-Holland is a teacher, poet, dog-lover, who loves to see others' poetry dreams materialize. After nearly sixty years with her lifelong partner, Fran is now dedicating herself to poetry in both a personal and larger sense. She is grateful for the community that surrounds her and sustains her in her years not of retirement, but of heartfelt engagement with close friends and the poetry group that continues to meet weekly despite the pandemic. Recently, she has found Zoom a way to stay in touch with her poetry group and thanks the wonderful poets for being patient when she slips into her teacher mode.

Fran Claggett, after many years of teaching at the high school and university levels, devoted a number of years teaching poetry and memoir writing in the Osher Lifelong Learning Institute at Sonoma State University. During her rich post-teaching years, Fran gave workshops throughout the country, as well as in Guam, Panama and the Virgin Islands through the Bay Area Writing Project. Fran's interest in brain research led her to develop approaches to reading , writing, and thinking using metaphorical graphics. She has received many awards for her teaching and writing, including the Lifetime Achievement Award from the California Association of Teachers of English.

Fran has either written or co-written a number of books for teachers, including Teaching Writing: Craft, Art, Genre; Drawing Your Own Conclusions: Graphic Strategies for Reading, Writing, and Thinking, with Joan Brown; A Measure of Success: From Assignment to Assessment in English Language Arts (winner of the James N. Britton Award). With Louann Reid and Ruth Vinz, she wrote Learning the Landscape and Recasting the Text, as well as the comprehensive Daybooks of Critical Reading and Writing, an innovative set of texts for middle, high school, and JC students, integrating critical reading, writing, and thinking. Fran's current book, Under the Wings of the Crow, includes new poems, and poems selected from previous collections-- Black Birds and Other Birds (Taurean Horn Press), Crow Crossings, and The Consciousness of Stone (both RiskPress) and Moments with Madge: Lux Aeterna (the White Crow Press).

Acknowledgements

First I want to acknowledge this wonderful, supportive artistic community. To live among poets, artists, and musicians and to know so many of you as friends is a rare privilege, one which I do not take lightly. It has made my life these last eight years not only possible, but fulfilling in a way I could not have imagined. If you are reading this book, you have helped create it. It is that simple. It is that profound.

The two poetry groups that meet weekly provide an ongoing focus for me, as poetry has become the central activity in my life. In the face of this overwhelming pandemic we are still living through, Zoom has created an opportunity to continue these powerful groups and even extend our opportunities to meet with other groups. Most important, however, is the trust we have developed as we offer our poems, and through our poems, our lives, to each other in our commitment to our art.

I want to pay special tribute to my two spiritual sons--Michael Franco and Freeman Ng, who demonstrate unwavering dedication to their lives of poetry and art. Michael, from Massachusetts, and Freeman, now of St. Paul, have been my inspiration for years. I am fortunate to have known and loved them for going on fifty years, ever since they were promising neophyte poets in my classroom.

Once again, I am deeply indebted to Charlie Pendergast and Kevin Connor, who took my pages of poems and turned them into this book. Their generosity and skill in book design have made this book possible.

In keeping with the tradition begun by Charlie to support our artistic community, the proceeds of the sales of this book will go to the Sebastopol Center for the Arts.

Words from Friends

At the Far End of a Sturdy Branch
for Fran Claggett-Holland

You,
    who knew Robert Frost,
    and bought a Picasso
    with money you didn't have,
now greet me at your door
with a Saluki and a Whippet,
in a dress windswept
with charcoal brush strokes,
a necklace which only
your neck could honor,
and a smile to welcome me in.

The house brims with art.
A collusion of couches and chairs
brace themselves to accommodate
an entire tribe of poets.
The butcher block, scored
with decades of Madge's slices
in concert with flour from your hands.

As you speak of your two only sons,
both poets grown grey,
and Madge behind a permeable
membrane of memory—
I hear the music of
"the end of your beginning,
measuring out the days
grounded in rhythm and rhyme."

At one point I envision you
holding a cup of hot chocolate,
marshmallows melting on the surface,
afloat on the second movement
of Beethoven's Pathetique.

While you leave a lifetime
of astonished poets in your wake,
(every encounter a potential student)
I catch a glimpse of what
my life could have been,
and might still become.

Steve Trenam

The first time I read Fran Claggett-Holland's poetry, the humanity of it spun me like a dreidel where wisdom is embedded in the letters. She writes from the space between scholarship and heart, mystery and truth. Reading her intensifies awareness of those spaces within ourselves. This book, Under the Wings of the Crow, is the chance for everyone to know and love her as I do."
~*Gale Kissin*

Traversing classical to modern poetic forms, Fran effortlessly weaves authentic feelings and spiritual realities into a delightful tapestry of words.
~*Warren Bellows*

Fran Claggett-Holland's authentic accessible poetry will invite you to cry, laugh, think, change and engage fully with the human experience. The values she lives by, reflected in her written words, have changed my life. They will change yours too.
~*Jo Ann Smith*

Fran Claggett-Holland writes beautiful poems that sculpt in light the moments of awakening and memory, the times of loss and reckoning. Her voice is clear, contemplative, at times oracular, always authentic in its journey toward the essence of things. She would "write a poem for you, without time or distance" or one "hidden in a potted orchid." In her poetry, she can ride a fresh thought into bright being, reveal deep spiritual truth about our relationships with objects and others, trees and friendship, crows, and love, and capture the delicate balance of a child's view of death. Her poems create a network of rousing and vital associations that nourish and revive us. She guides us into the expansive halls of poetry and opens all the windows.
~*Margaret Rooney*

The Irish claim there's wisdom in a raven's head.
Her eye is keen, her wingbeats, relaxed and confident.
She has an impressive array of vocalizations:
from the heart but grounded in music, myth, and science.
She knows how to stir the "kettle." So it is with
Fran Claggett-Holland---trusted mentor, gifted poet,
no ordinary bird, for sure.
~*Barbara Armstrong*

Fran Claggett-Holland is an extraordinary poet and teacher. To encounter Fran, to get to know her, is to come away astonished and enriched. So it is with Fran's poems. They will touch your heart and mind and you'll want to come back to them over and over, like old friends. "Under the Wings of the Crow" is a special treat, bringing so many of Fran's poems under one cover, inviting readers in to experience life seen through the eyes of this remarkable poet.
~*Betty Les*

Afterword

Under the Wing of the Crow

Under the wing of the Crow
the wind is Everywhere
the earth falls away

to where

silence is an observation
or an intent or even a small hop toward
where everything's necessary
and shelter carries intent small
and clutched in its beak toward
the fulfilment of nest or egg or firm lodging
against all manner of storm
and calls out

emerging   as a practice and a fulfilment
known only in

the flutter of a wing

arrival

Michael Franco

In the turns made along the Path of any life in Poetry there are alleyways
and small streets, calling the possibility of adventure .....I have traveled
many of these, have in both my own Work and Daily Living found my
Self so often lost or staring at yet another dead end found in the abrupt
dissolution of yet another grand idea proposed...

At some point in my 20's, still not so far away in Time's meander-
ing silence from my time as a student of Fran Claggett-Holland, (Miss
Claggett as I then knew her), I began to understand as I turned to look
back that she was still there with me, still setting the Measure of a Life in
Poetry still guiding still Calling me to Continue. As I have grown older
....indeed older now by far than she was at that time when I was first her
student, I have come in that rare way to Know her, to See, that within her
Work, within her Life at Work in the Work, that she has held those of us
who would read and study her, who would know her, Here; precise and
open in the twists and excitements of her Language; of her own life at
work in Language and the Poetry of that language as it wings its way to
the composing Poem of that Life.

...Indeed I have found myself alone and lost in the confusion and yet in turning in preparing to start out yet again, always there is in the far distance there is a light that calls and guides my return to begin again and always that Light has been from Fran Claggett-Holland.

It is then without exaggeration a moment of Clarity to say that it is her Life at Work that has held so many of us as we have crossed what suddenly became decades. It is also without exaggeration that I would say that while I was a student of Fran Claggett-Holland, each day without exception, at some point I am reminded that I Am a Student of the Poem that is Fran Claggett-Holland: Immeasurable then Under the Wings of the Crow here in the deep Measures of this ongoing Book.

Michael Franco

This book was set in 10 point Palatino Linotype
Designed by Charlie Pendergast and Kevin Connor
Printed in the United States

Made in the USA
Middletown, DE
27 April 2022

64810619R00083